STILLNESS
A Guide to Finding Your Inner Peace

Joseph P. Kauffman

conscious-collective.com

ISBN-13: 978-1534938588
ISBN-10: 1534938583

Stillness

DEDICATION

This book is dedicated to all of those who seek to find peace in their lives, and to those who seek to bring peace to the world. World peace will only be possible once each one of us has found inner peace.

~

Stillness

CONTENTS

INTRODUCTION

*"The first peace, which is the most important, is that
which comes within the souls of people when they
realize their relationship, their oneness, with the
universe and all its powers, and when they realize that
at the center of the universe dwells the Great Spirit,
and that this center is really everywhere, it is within
each of us."*
— *Black Elk*

Most people view the world as something that exists separately from them. They feel like they are alone in this world, like they are victims, like they don't belong. They experience life with pervasive feelings of lack, anxiety, and discontentment, and they constantly try to escape these painful feelings through different sources of entertainment, pleasure, drugs, and other types of stimulating distractions. Though once every stimulating experience comes to an end, the feelings of lack and discomfort return, and the suffering still remains.

Over the years, various religions and philosophies have tried to cure this sense of emptiness from our lives by promising us a better life after death. Marketers say that we will find the cure in the products they have to offer—in material objects. Society has fooled most people into thinking that it will come from financial wealth, and numerous others have suggested their relief from this troubling sense of discontentment in their own distinctive ways.

Believing that these short-lived distractions might hold the key to filling the emptiness in our lives, we go off in pursuit of pleasure and happiness, fruitlessly attempting to find it in products, experiences, and relationships—none of which have been successful in providing us with lasting peace and fulfilment—and that is because we have not yet developed peace within ourselves.

We do not have to wait until we die, until we find our significant other, until we have enough money, or until we have our desired lifestyle, to experience peace. We can experience peace right here and now; all we have to do is realize who we are at our deepest level.

Inner peace comes to us when we are aware of our true nature, and when we learn to live in harmony with the truth of our being, rather than resisting it and living against it. Ignorance of our true nature is what produces all of our suffering.

We are not insignificant creatures living in a mechanical and dispassionate universe, contrary to what many believe. We are divine expressions of the whole of existence—the entire universe is expressing itself through our being.

Failing to realize who we are, we go on an endless search for fulfilment. But peace will not come from searching outside of ourselves for satisfaction. In order to find peace in our lives, we need to turn our attention inward. This book is a guide to assist you in this process of self-examination, so that you may awaken to your true nature, and experience the peace that this knowledge provides.

The concepts discussed in this book are not entirely my own; they are based on the spiritual teachings of ancient cultures and world religions, and on new discoveries in quantum physics and modern science. This book is simply my translation of an ancient truth, written in hopes that it will enable many more people to understand it so that they, too, can experience the peace that this ancient truth provides.

I would like to mention that by no means do I think that I have all the answers. I can only speak for what is true for my experience; you have to determine what is true for yours. My hope is that I can share the knowledge that I have gained from my experience in order to help you find peace in your own life experience.

It is my understanding that peace comes to us when we have a deep understanding of ourselves and our existence, and when we learn to stop identifying with the things that are not essentially us, and thus stop being so emotionally attached and stressed over these things.

If you want to be at peace, and want to see the greater reality that spiritual masters and ancient mystics have spoken of for millennia, then allow this book to help you remember who you are and just how valuable your existence is.

If there is something in this book that you do not understand, please do not try too hard or strain to comprehend it. Just let the words enter your mind calmly as if you were listening to a peaceful melody. Allow these words to bring you to a greater understanding of life and help you find joy in your experience; allow these words to bring you peace.

Stillness

1 EMPTYING YOUR MIND

Our minds are full—full of opinions, beliefs, judgments, memories, and thoughts; full of concepts about what we think the world is, what it isn't, what is right and what is wrong; full of opinions about who we think we are, what we can accomplish, and what we can and can't achieve; and full of the experiences that we have accumulated throughout our lives that have shaped our perceptions of reality into what we think of it today.

We live according to these accumulated beliefs, we base our worldviews on them, and we set our limitations on life according to them. But what if our beliefs are wrong? What if the things we have been taught, the opinions that we hold on to so strongly, or the concepts we have been given to define our experience, are untrue?

What if we have been living our entire lives, thinking in a way that was actually far from the truth? What if our history books, our scientific theories, our religious beliefs— what if they are all wrong?

I am not suggesting that they are, but how do we know for sure? Did you discover these concepts for yourself? Did you witness them? Did you come to your own conclusions on life based on your own experience?

Or were you taught what to think about life? Did you adopt your worldviews from the worldviews of others? And if so, where did they get their beliefs? Did they adopt them from others just as you did, only a generation sooner?

Our entire culture lives based on the opinions and experiences of other people. We read about life through textbooks, we watch it through a television screen, we hear about it from our elders, but how much do we know about life that comes from our own experiences, our own realizations of truth and our own perspectives?

The common perception of society is not one that allows much room for curiosity, questioning, or imagination. Everyone acts so sure of their opinions and they are quick to defend themselves if their opinions are questioned.

Most people attempt to live life "realistically," according to the beliefs that are shared by the majority of people. Anyone that even suggests that the truth of life may be different than what we have been taught is often dismissed as "crazy," "weird," or a "conspiracy theorist." People love their beliefs and they don't even want to consider the notion that their beloved beliefs might be wrong, so they are quick to condemn something they don't understand or something that contradicts their current way of thinking.

As much as people cling to their beliefs and opinions about life, and about what they think this experience is, many people remain rather unhappy with the life that they live. So many people feel sad, lonely, anxious, stressed, fearful, and isolated.

It is likely that even you feel this way, and perhaps that is why you are interested in a book that teaches you how to find your inner peace.

The beliefs that you cling to, your perspective on life, and the thoughts that you think of the world, haven't served you well enough in the past to give you lasting joy and peace, so why not consider letting go of them, and learning to see reality from a new perspective, your own perspective, not one given to you by your culture?

Our perception is our window to the world, and we need to wipe the dust off of our window often so we can continue to see through it clearly. When we cling to beliefs and opinions without ever changing them, we cease to grow; we become dull, stiff, and bitter. Remaining open minded to new concepts allows us to experience life with more clarity.

This book is one that may or may not require you to leave behind your current worldviews and opinions, but regardless it should be read by a mind that is open and free. The only way we can grow is if we change, no matter how uncomfortable it may seem at the time.

This information can help you find your own inner peace, but it cannot be forced upon you; it can only be received if you are open to receiving it.

If you are ready to leave behind your suffering and embrace a new reality, then empty your mind of the beliefs and opinions that fill it, let go of the thoughts that take away your joy, and learn to see reality from a new perspective— from your own perspective. Let yourself discover how peaceful and joyful your life can really be.

> *"Empty your cup so that it may be filled; become devoid to gain totality."*
> — *Bruce Lee*

Stillness

2 CULTURAL CONDITIONING

Before discussing how you can find your inner peace, you should have a clear understanding of your inner world—your awareness, thoughts, feelings, and perceptions.

Reflecting on your upbringing will help you understand why you think the way that you do today, and will allow you to let go of the beliefs that no longer serve you, so you can discover the truth about your existence from your own unique perspective.

When you were born, your mind was empty. You had no knowledge of who you were, where you had come from, or where you were going. You had no fears, worries, or doubts; no sadness, depression or anxiety; you just were. With no prior influence or sensory input from the outer world, your mind was vacant, like a blank white canvas, yet to be colored by an artist.

Then as you came into contact with your surroundings, things began to fill your empty mind. Thousands of different sights, sounds, scents, tastes, feelings and sensations, all making their way into your experience, imprinting their own unique mark on your fragile, unprotected awareness.

Over time, this caused you to develop certain beliefs about life based on your experiences, along with certain beliefs about who you are. The genes in your DNA did all of the work up until birth, but from that point on you were a product of your environment. That is why some people speak Japanese, some speak English, others speak Spanish, and a multitude of different languages all reflecting the culture that the person was raised in.

That is why someone born in New York is likely to be more interested in journalism, business, or fashion, while someone born in Costa Rica may be more interested in farming, hiking, or surfing. The things that surround you have a huge influence on your behavior—everything from the movies you watch, and the people you spend time with, to the foods that you eat and the books that you read. Each thing that comes into contact with your awareness plays a significant role in determining your perception of reality.

The culture that you were raised in conditioned your mind to think according to the common perception of that culture. This mental conditioning creates a type of prison for you, by setting the limits on how you perceive your reality.

At a certain age, you began to consciously ignore, accept, or reject the information that entered your experience. Though in your primal stages of development, you were vulnerable, completely susceptible to your environment and a victim of the influence of your culture. Some people, regardless of age, never make it past this mental barrier and are always victims of their surroundings, forever falling prey to the opinions and influences of other people.

Looking at our development in this way, we can see that at birth, each of our minds were empty—nothing but pure consciousness; a blank state of awareness. Then, our culture began filling our minds with information that varied according to our individual experiences. As a result, each of us perceives reality differently.

Just as you can fill a blank canvas with any variation of color, you can fill an empty mind with any variation of information and beliefs, whether they are of violence or peace. No child was born with hatred, racism, or prejudice—these were learned by our culture.

When you were young, someone you were around—whether it was a family figure, childhood friend, or an actor on the television screen—portrayed a destructive form of behavior, and you adopted or emulated that behavior. Of course this didn't happen only once, it was a very involved process, where everything you observed played a part in conditioning your mind.

Every individual exists under different circumstances, and so, each person experiences life uniquely. But regardless of circumstances, in the early years of a person's development, their minds are like a sponge, absorbing everything around them without any filter to distinguish the wholesome behaviors from the unwholesome. We had no control over the information we received in our years as infants, and whatever experiences we had contributed to our education.

The environments we are raised in as children program our minds accordingly. Whether we are influenced by peaceful or violent actions, intelligent or ignorant knowledge, selfless or selfish attitudes, our minds adopt those qualities.

When you went to school, the teacher told you that their perception was correct, and that your point of view was incorrect. You were rewarded for complying and punished for disobeying. This is likely how you learned much of your sense for what is "right" or "wrong"—you learned what was socially acceptable, and what was socially offensive.

If you went to church, you might recall the pastor speaking strongly about their knowledge of God, perhaps shaping your beliefs accordingly. And if your family and friends shared the same beliefs, that only strengthened the notion that these beliefs were the absolute truth.

When you watched a television program, it portrayed certain behaviors to you and you were given a glimpse of how your culture thinks and acts. The television *programmed* a part of your behavior.

When you were at home or day care, you asked an adult what "this" was, what "that" was and so you began to define your surroundings and classify each object into its own separate box: "mom, dad, table, chair, couch, etc." and this is the very same language that you are using today.

You think in this language, you speak in this language, but you did not create it. It was given to you by your culture, as were most of the thoughts you think, and behaviors you act out. Very few of your thoughts are your own, and even fewer if you have no awareness of this cultural conditioning.

Our worldviews, beliefs, and states of mind are a reflection of our experiences and our cultural conditioning. Every friend, relative, and person, each television show, video, and game, every doctor's visit, road trip, meal eaten, and car driven, every sight, sound, and sensation we are exposed to, every experience we have ever had, has influenced our minds into thinking the way that we think today.

Our society has set many standards for the behavior that is expected and the perspective that is considered correct, and due to our indoctrination in society, we also have been molded to think and behave according to these standards.

As a result of our established way of thinking, we have been trained to always define, explain, and categorize every experience into its own separate box. Our minds like to label things, give them names, and organize them. Though we fail to realize that in doing this, we separate things, when in reality nothing is separate.

3 REALIZING THE CONNECTION BETWEEN EVERYTHING

*"Only words and conventions can isolate us
from the entirely undefinable something which
is everything."*
– Alan Watts

As children being taught a new language, we are ignorant to the restrictions of verbal communication. Though eventually, most of us come to realize that there are certain things that language and thought do not have the ability to explain.

The universe is too vast and complex to be defined by words, and the harder we try to describe it, the more we separate ourselves from our experience. Life is something that has to be lived, not explained.

We spend so much of our time lost in thought, trying to label everything as isolated objects and events. Though we fail to realize that our thoughts are incapable of defining anything in its totality. We can think about a situation for as long as we want to, but our thoughts will never know the situation exactly as it exists.

When we think of something, we create a mental image of it, and our image is then always filtered through our mental perception. We may meet someone one day when they are in a bad mood, we then make a false assumption that this person is mean or unkind. We have created an image of this person, and now every time we meet them, we associate this person with our negative mental image of them. We don't interact with them as they are in this moment; we interact with how we think they are.

Much of our suffering is caused by our false perceptions and attachment to mental images. We assume things to be true without really knowing whether they are true or not, then create a world of hurt for ourselves and others.

Many people have failing relationships because they have not really fallen in love with each other, but they have fallen for the mental images they have created of one another. We assume we know our partner, we think about them nonstop, creating many different ideas of who they are, what they like, and how we will be together, then as soon as our partner does something that doesn't fit with our mental image of them, we become sad, upset, confused, or heart broken. Our partner did not cause our suffering; we caused it, through our false perceptions and mental images.

We spend so much time dwelling on our thoughts, wanting everything to be known, defined, and understood. This way of thinking was imposed upon us at an early age, so to us it seems natural. Though it is far from natural. It is an addiction to thought that we have adopted from our culture, but because of our familiarity with this addiction, we do not recognize its presence, or the harm it inflicts upon our mental and emotional health.

The majority of our thoughts only take us away from experiencing the present moment. They cannot understand the moment as it exists, they can only create mental images of the moment, and give us a false perception of what this moment is.

To experience things as they exist, we have to let go of our thoughts and our need to define everything, and understand that life cannot be defined, only lived. Everything in existence is existing together, as one entity. Thoughts as well as the language that we think them in, can only comprehend specific parts of nature, not nature as a whole.

In order to give a name to something, we have to separate it from everything else. For example, when we give a name to a tree, we separate the tree from everything that the tree is a part of. We separate the tree from the soil, the soil from the rock, the rock from the earth, etc. failing to acknowledge that all of these things exist together.

The name "tree" is not a tree itself; it is just a word, a sound, a vibration. The name is not really the thing that we attempt to define as a "tree," and in order to label it as a "tree" we have to assume that the tree has an independent existence, apart from its environment.

In our attempt to define nature with words, our minds have only classified nature into many separate mental categories. It is impossible to name nature without dividing it, because nature itself is one living entity that remains undivided.

A tree is constantly taking in the sun, the air, the rain and the earth. A world of energy moves in and out of this thing we call a "tree." Billions of organisms and bacteria crawling on its surface and fertilizing the soil allowing the tree to grow, unimaginable amounts of different interactions occurring on nearly every level. A tree is not a static object; it is an event of frequent change.

We couldn't possibly understand this organism in its totality, making it useful to classify it as a "tree" for purposes of communication, but to mistake this living organism for our static classification of it is completely irrational. In fact, if we look deeply enough we will see that there is no actual boundary separating the tree from everything we consider to be not a tree.

The tree is not separate from the earth of which it grows. Just as the earth, the air, the water, and the sky are not separate from one another or the universe in which they exist. There is no possibility of a tree growing without soil or the minerals needed to nourish its growth, just as there is no possibility of soil existing without the things that make up what we call "soil"—trillions of microorganisms, organic matter, and rock particles.

These things could not exist without the earth from which they came, nor could the earth exist without its delicate balance in the solar system, the solar system's balance in the galaxy, or the galaxy's balance in the universe.

Looking deeply in this way, we see that nature is whole, and it is only our language and thought which have attempted to divide nature, though nothing in nature exists as a separate individual, apart from its environment.

Because of our illusory way of thinking, we tend to go through life labeling each experience, classifying it, organizing it in our minds. But the experience itself is so vast and so detailed that we couldn't possibly categorize it with our limited language. So rather than experiencing life, we try to define our experience of life, but our definitions of life always fall short of the life that we are experiencing.

In our attempt to endlessly define nature, we have been unable to define ourselves, which leaves us feeling lost and confused. Our confusion is produced by our failure to realize that there is no individual "self" that we can define, as all things, no matter how unique they may be, are ultimately connected to the greater whole of the universe.

Because of our conditioning, we have developed the idea that we are separate entities. We truly think and feel that we exist independently of the world around us. We have created a mental image of who we are, and we cling to this image for a sense of identity, but our image of ourselves is not who we really are, it is just an illusion that our mind has created.

The electrons vibrating in each atom of your being are also connected to the subatomic particles that comprise every plant that grows, every fish that swims, and every star that illuminates the sky. Nature in its totality, including ourselves, is indivisible. We are not separate from the universe; we are the universe.

A human being only exists because of non-human elements. We depend on our environment to sustain us. It is because of the trees, the rivers, the oceans, the air, the sun, the earth, heat, food, etc. that we exist. We could not exist without these elements.

So why do we each perceive ourselves as "I" and look to the world as if it was something separate from "I," as if it were our enemy? We think that we exist within this skin, and everything outside of our skin is something separate from us.

We act as if we exist in the universe and are not of this universe. We say we were born on this planet and are not of this planet, when all of the elements in our being were provided by the stars, and every cell in our body came from the earth.

Our feeling of separation comes from a lack of understanding our true nature. We have identified ourselves with the ego—a mental image created by the mind. We are now in a constant search for what can validate our existence as this imagined entity, but no matter how hard we look, we will never find anything to satisfy this illusory way of thinking. Our entire society suffers from this illusion, and over the course of our upbringing we have adopted it as well.

Rather than looking into this illusion, most people are unaware of it. They allow it to guide them through life, and they avoid anything that may cause them to confront it. The illusions created by the mind are incapable of understanding the truth of life.

The mind has tried to identify itself and its experience with labels, definitions, and names—products of thought that do not exist in reality—though the truth of our being is so vast and incomprehensible that it cannot be conceived by thought or defined by language, it can only be experienced as it exists in this moment.

4 UNDERSTANDING OUR TRUE NATURE

If I were to ask you right now, "who are you?" How would you respond? Would you respond by telling me your name? Your occupation? Your education? Your ethnicity, your personal history, your accomplishments or your beliefs?

Do you really feel like any of these define *you*? All of these descriptions are nothing but information that we have accumulated over the course of our development, but who are you at the very core of your being?

You are not your body. Your body is undergoing continuous change, being fed and fueled by things that are not your body—food, water, sunlight, air, etc. Without these elements, your body cannot exist. Not to mention that the body you have now is not at all the same body that you had at birth. Indeed, the only true body that exists is the entire interconnected universe.

You are not your thoughts or feelings either. Your thoughts and feelings change just as constantly as anything else in the universe. One moment you may think a positive thought and feel happy, then the next moment you may think a negative thought and feel miserable. If there is always a you preceding every thought and feeling, how can your thoughts and emotions be you?

You are not your name. Your name is just a label given to you by society. We may identify with this name, but the true you cannot be confined to a label. Besides, you could have been given any name. Your name is not who you are.

Neither are you your education, your job, or your position in society. These are just roles that we identify with, but these roles change constantly. They are not who you are.

You are not your personality or the image of yourself that you created based on your personal history. The memories you use to form an image of your life story are just information that has been stored by your mind. We may think of our memories of the past, but we only remember very minor details of what actually happened. So we can use these minor details stored in our memory to form an image of who we are, but the reality of who we are is far beyond our personal image.

So if you are not your body, your thoughts, your feelings, your name, your education, your job, your position in society, your personality, your history, or your self-image, then who are you?

Just as you have always been, before your culture conditioned you to believe otherwise, you are this consciousness experiencing reality right now. You are the awareness that is perceiving these words and turning them into thoughts—the awareness that creates the world with every act of observation. Without this awareness, there would be no reality, no perception, no thoughts, and no world.

How could anything exist without an awareness to acknowledge its existence? Who would be there to know whether or not it existed? Everything that happens occurs within the field of awareness. This awareness is our deepest level of being.

This awareness is the real you that is unchanging, formless, and eternal. It is the you that remains the same regardless of changing circumstances.

We have been conditioned to identify with things that are not essentially us, causing us to be very confused about our existence. We have been taught to identify with forms that are undergoing continuous change, though our true nature is awareness, and it is formless.

Throughout your entire life your circumstances are constantly changing, yet the awareness witnessing all of these circumstances doesn't change. We are always present throughout all of life's experiences, so it shouldn't be much of a surprise to discover that your true nature is the awareness in which experience happens.

As simple as it is, most people have difficulty accepting this information because of their identification with their body and their overactive mind. We feel this presence, we are aware of our existence, but we can't find the thoughts or the words to explain our existence, and so we feel confused and perhaps even frustrated. Our frustration is caused by trying to define the undefinable. We want to define consciousness, though consciousness cannot be the object of its own knowledge, as consciousness is not an object, it is a subjective experience; it is the essence of who we are.

Nothing can exist without consciousness. This is not only a statement of profound spiritual importance; it is a statement of immense scientific importance as well.

Consciousness is not something brought about by physical matter, contrary to what most people believe. Consciousness is what creates physical matter. There can be no matter without consciousness.[1]

---

[1] http://www.collective-evolution.com/2014/11/11/consciousness-creates-reality-physicists-admit-the-universe-is-immaterial-mental-spiritual/

According to the leading edge discoveries in quantum physics, without an observer, there is no Universe. The Double Slit Experiment—an experiment replicated by many different physicists—proves to us that all matter exists as waves of energy, and only when there is an observer present do the waves collapse into particles of physical matter.

In fact, what we call physical matter is not really physical at all. Science has also proven that every single atom is made up of 99.9999999999999% empty space. If you could somehow remove all the empty space out of all the atoms in all the people in the world, you would be able to fit the entire human race in the volume of a sugar cube.[2] Physical matter is nothing but an illusion that operates in relation to our sensory perception.

> *"As a man who has devoted his whole life to the most clearheaded science, to the study of matter, I can tell you as a result of my research about atoms this much: there is no matter as such. All matter originates and exists only by virtue of a force which brings the particles of an atom to vibration and holds this most minute solar system of the atom together. We must assume behind this force the existence of a conscious and intelligent Mind. This Mind is the matrix of all matter."*
> *– Max Planck, Nobel Prize–winning Physicist*

We are creating the world with every act of observation. From the view of separateness this does not seem to make any sense. How could I be creating the world with every act of observation, if it is evident that you have an existence independent of mine?

---

[2] http://www.physics.org/featuredetail.asp?id=41

It is possible because your existence is not separate from mine. There is no separation. We are creating this world together. The source of consciousness within you is the very same source of consciousness that exists within me. Really, we are one. We only appear to have a separate existence because of the many different forms that our consciousness inhabits.

Each form has its own attributes, its own senses, its own perception, and its own experience. Yet the substance of experience—the consciousness that allows any experience to happen at all—is the same in all things. The formless nature of consciousness is an essential requirement for the existence of varying physical forms. You are not a body with consciousness; you are consciousness with a body.

Everything is just energy dancing in form, and this dance is a continuous merging of the form with the formless. Hindu and Buddhist philosophy has understood this truth for thousands of years, and modern science is now beginning to confirm it.

You can find all the evidence you need to support this theory online or in the studies of quantum mechanics, but you need only to look within yourself to know that it is the truth. This is the way that the ancients discovered it, long before there existed instruments capable of studying matter at the quantum level.

This knowledge was not obtained by them through intellectual conceptualization or analysis; it was gained through their direct experience of their most essential nature. Rather than looking out into the universe for guidance and understanding, they looked deeply within themselves.

In order to come to your own realization of this truth, you must be willing to see things as they are, rather than as you have been taught to see them. This means that you must be willing to transcend the conditioned mind as well as the thoughts that it projects, as thoughts are limited to our language and memory.

Just as the totality of nature is too vast to be understood by thought, this awareness cannot be comprehended by the thinking mind, since it is this awareness that produces the thinking mind. This awareness is so immense, so alive, and so profound, that the only way we can truly know it is to give up trying to define it, and simply be it as it exists in this moment.

Life Is Happening Now

The only moment that ever exists is this moment. We typically think that life is a collection of many moments, in which thousands of different things are happening. Yet, when we look at our experience clearly, we see that life is only ever happening now.

We can think back to our memory of the past, but our memory is still something happening in this moment; and we can create images of the future, but when the future comes, it will still be this moment. The present moment is the only thing that we can never escape. No matter what happens, it will always be happening now.

The only thing that remains consistent in the present moment is our awareness. Life's situations and circumstances are constantly changing, but the awareness that these situations and circumstances occur in remains the same.

When we lose touch with the present moment, and our awareness is lost in thoughts of tomorrow or memories of yesterday, we begin to lose touch with ourselves. The longer we are lost in thought, the less we feel secure in who we are. In order to return to ourselves, we have to return our awareness back to the present moment.

Awareness and the present moment are inseparable. No matter how hard we try, we cannot find any part of us that exists apart from the experience of this moment. There is no object without a subject, nor is the subject separate from the object. When you look at a flower, the flower is the object of your perception—it is also you. To perceive always means to perceive something.

When we perceive the stars, the stars are in us. When we perceive our friend, our friend is also in us. There is no perception without an object of perception. The observer is not separate from the object observed.

There is nothing that can exist outside of the field of awareness. When we are conscious of a tree, the tree is our consciousness. The idea that our consciousness exists outside of the tree has to be removed. The notion that there is a separate "I" existing apart from this experience is just an illusion created by the mind, and this illusion is the cause of our suffering.

We associate our memory, any painful incidents, embarrassing moments, or traumatic experiences with "I." We create mental images of these past events and associate these images with who we are. Even though the experience has gone, we still hold onto it. Our failure to let go of the past and live in the present is the only reason that we ever feel sad, miserable, or depressed.

Our attachment to our past experiences makes us feel as if we are victims of the world, that we don't belong. Though again, this is all the cause of a mental image and false perception created by our thinking mind. In reality, we are the world and we not only belong, but we are an essential part of the greater whole. There is nothing that remains unaffected by our existence, as all things are connected at their deepest level.

"I" Is Just a Thought

Can you find an "I" that exists separately from this present experience? In other words, can you read this sentence and be aware of yourself reading it? In order to think the thought "I am reading," you have to stop reading. So then, the experience of thought is your experience, not the experience of reading, and it is still an experience happening now, in the present moment.

The present moment is the only moment that exists, and it is constantly changing. Our thoughts cannot understand the present moment, for as soon as we think about it, the moment at which we began thinking has already passed.

The only way to catch up to the speed of life is to flow with it. The present moment changes so constantly, that we can only know it by experiencing it exactly as it exists now. We have to go with the change of the moment rather than resist it.

Do you think that the water of a river ever resists its flow? What do you think would happen if it did? It would fight against itself until it was no longer capable of resisting, and it would be forced to surrender to the flow of the river.

The present moment is always changing, flowing just like a river. When we resist our experience in the present moment, we create our own suffering until we have no choice but to let go of our struggle.

The present moment is so vast, and changes so quickly, that there is no way we can understand it; we just have to flow with the change.

Just like the present moment, our awareness is incomprehensible by the thinking mind, and so in order to understand our true selves, we have to be our true selves— we have to be totally aware of life as a whole, without our minds trying to understand it, divide it, label it, or judge it.

We cannot be aware of awareness, just as we cannot see our eyes, hear our ears, or taste our tongue. The only way to know the nature of awareness is to be awareness itself. The only way to be ourselves is to be—without any self-conscious thoughts of who, what, why, or how to be.

As soon as we try to label our experience or comprehend it with our minds, we separate ourselves from the reality of the moment and become lost in thought.

The mind has a desire to know, understand and control everything. The present moment is unknowable, incomprehensible, and uncontrollable. The mind cannot know the present moment, which is always new and always changing, and so it fears the present moment and constantly tries to escape it.

The present moment is something that we can never escape, and in its attempt to escape it, the mind has created a false sense of identity—one that it can know, understand and feel safe with. This illusory identity is known as "the ego."

The ego is not who we are, it is who we think we are. When we think of our name, our image, our history, and our life experiences as who we are, we become associated with an idea of ourselves, a mental image that is not at all who we really are at our core.

Stillness

5 THE EGO

The ego is our self-image; it is not our true self. It is an illusion created by the mind—the idea of an "I" that feels and exists separately from the rest of the Universe.

We all have an image of who we are, how we think of ourselves, and how we think others perceive us, but this image is not really who we are; it is just an illusion.

Our true nature is awareness. It is being. It is not something that we can make up, it is not something that changes according to our different moods and opinions. It just is.

When we are identified with the illusion of our self-image, we do all kinds of strange and unnecessary things just to maintain it. We feel the need to always state our point of view, push our beliefs onto others, tell them about our experiences, tell them who we are, what we like, what we dislike, and so on...always focused on "me."

As long as we continue to try to maintain this mental image, we will never know ourselves to be the awareness that witnesses the mental image. All we have to do to see through the illusion of this mental image is stop trying to maintain it.

If we stop completely, not just outwardly, but inwardly, we will see that there is no truth to our self-image; it is completely mind-made. We cling so tightly to this illusory image because we believe it to be who we are, though it requires much more effort (and produces much more suffering) to always maintain this image and fear for its protection, than it does to just accept its illusory nature.

Surrendering our idea of ourselves will not make us disappear; we will just return to our true nature and live life grounded in our being, instead of living it lost in our thoughts.

Life is much simpler when we live in harmony with who we really are, rather than trying to live according to who we think we are, or how we think we should be. The only reason we have difficulty with doing this is because we do not really know who we are, and that is because we are trying to understand the whole of our existence with the fragmented perspective of our intellectual mind.

All we have to do to know ourselves is be ourselves, and live naturally in each moment of our lives. Unfortunately, this is a task that is difficult for most people, as we have been conditioned to live according to society's standards, rather than according to our own essential nature.

The ego comes about as an association between the presence of consciousness and the body. When the mind first forms this association, it gives birth to the idea that it has an existence of its own. When this idea develops, it draws our attention away from our true self, thus we easily forget who we are.

Because our society is supportive of the ego, we are not taught to reconnect with our true self after this association has formed, causing the binds of the ego to grow even stronger.

The ego is neither good nor bad. It is just an association that the mind has made between consciousness and the body. It is an illusion, meaning it only has as much power as we give to it. The problem lies not in the fact that the mind has created the ego, but in our mistaking the ego for who we are, rather than understanding our existence as consciousness—the awareness in which the ego arises.

Identification with the ego makes us bound to the ego and produces our feelings of fear and insecurity. In order to free ourselves from the ego, all we need to do is realize who we are at our deepest level. Then we can learn to stop identifying with the ego, and stop being pushed around by its tendencies.

This requires more than just an intellectual understanding of the ego; it must also come from experience. Once you personally observe the illusory role of the ego in your own mind, only then will you be able to move beyond it and be free from it.

The ego is like a frightened child, always trying to ensure its safety and preserve its feeling of security and identity. The ego is bound to the mind and body, which are undergoing continuous change. Therefore, expecting to find security and lasting peace in the ego is like expecting to put out a fire with gasoline—it cannot be done.

There is no security in an illusory self-image which has no stability. The only true security and peace that we can find comes from releasing our identification with the ego, as well as with all temporary forms, and realizing our true identity as the formless source of awareness in which all forms arise.

Awareness is always present, and when we are grounded in our awareness we are at peace in the present moment. But when we are ignorant of our true nature—when we are identified with our thoughts—our mind is always trying to escape the present moment, thinking about the future, or clinging to the past. Hardly ever do we just be our natural selves in the moment without our thoughts interfering.

Because the mind cannot logically understand consciousness, it has attached itself to the idea of an "I" that it can understand—one that exists separately from its experience of the present moment. We compare our memory with our experience now and conclude that if "I" can be aware of the past and the present experience, then "I" must be something that is separate from these experiences. Though all of these thoughts are experiences happening right now in the eternity of the present moment.

The thinking mind cannot function when our attention is absorbed in the present, it can only function while dwelling on things that it is familiar with: words, ideas, images, and concepts of the past. As soon as we bring our awareness back into this moment, the thinking mind ceases to function.

Since the ego is a product of thought, it fears the present moment because it cannot exist in the present moment. The present moment is new, unknown, and always changing. The ego cannot know it because it is unknowable, and so it is constantly trying to escape into memory where it is familiar, known and "safe."

Even if our thoughts choose to dwell on something painful that happened in the past, the ego would prefer to dwell on it because it is still something familiar and known—something it can understand. The ego's biggest fear is the present moment, and when we are identified with the ego—with our thoughts and our ideas about ourselves—we, too, fear the present moment.

We fear the moment because we are unsure of who we are in this moment, so anytime we are faced with the present moment, we panic and quickly return back to thought where we have the illusion of safety and the concept of our separate self.

This is why so many people fear being alone. They can't stand the thought of being in the present moment without something or someone to help them escape it. So even when people are alone they are in a constant search for something that will distract them from just being – watching TV, listening to music, indulging in substances, playing on their phones, thinking endlessly.

People spend their entire lives trying to escape themselves. One of the most difficult things for any human being to accomplish is to be their complete natural self—without attempting to escape the experience through the entertainment of thought, the ingesting of substances, or the craving for sensory stimulation.

You can observe this uneasy tendency very easily in yourself. Try to stop completely. Stop all fears, all worries, all contemplation, all thoughts, all of the mind's illusions and fantasies; just completely stop and be alone in the silence of your natural state of being.

You will find that this is not at all as easy as it sounds. You may get a few glimpses of what it is like to stop and be completely still, but the experience is unlikely to last for more than a brief moment.

Does this not clearly display how delusional our way of thinking is? How extroverted and stimulated our mind is? We cannot even stand to be alone with ourselves for a few moments. Clearly this should give rise to the understanding of what causes our suffering.

We aren't content with who we are because we do not know who we are. We do not know who we are because we have never really been ourselves. We have always lost ourselves in the opinions of others, the stimulation of our senses, and the thoughts created by our mind.

The mind cannot know our most essential nature, as the mind is limited to the knowledge of its conditioned experience. To know yourself you have to be yourself. You cannot seek outside of yourself, asking questions about your existence and expecting to receive a satisfying answer. Rather than focusing on the answers, focus more on the one asking the questions.

The more you question who you are, the less sure you are of your existence. Eventually this makes the one asking the questions so uncomfortable that they have to stop asking. This is because it is the ego that is asking the questions.

The ego is trying to find its permanence in the world, which is ultimately an illusion. To follow the thought "Who am I?" to its conclusion would prove that the ego, or the thought of a separate "I" is just a product of the mind, something that has no stability. This would lead to the destruction of the ego, and since the ego fears its own demise, it will turn away from any questions that may reveal the truth about its illusory existence.

You are not the "I" that asks the questions; that is the ego. You are the awareness that precedes the ego, the awareness that allows the ego to even exist. You cannot know your nature as awareness by asking with the ego, you know it by being it, feeling it, and living it.

You are not a separate self. You have an individual experience because of the form that you currently inhabit— a form that is equipped with its own senses, and a brain to interpret these senses into a unique experience—but your existence is just as collective as it is individual.

All things have both a collective and an individual nature. Society is a collective of human experiences, but all of these experiences are felt and perceived individually.

You may have individual thoughts, but they are thought in a language that was given to you by society. This body is unique, yet it has been produced by the collective—your parents, ancestors, the food you eat, etc.

When we are angry, there is something in the collective that produced our anger. When we look deeply into nature, we can see that all things have both an individual and collective nature—to think things exist solely by themselves is an illusory perception.

A rose only exists because of the things that make up a rose. Your body only exists because of the things that make up it. Just as there is a heart within this body that gives us life, the sun is the cosmic heart that gives earth life—it gives us warmth, it allows plants to grow and produce the air that we breathe, and it produces the solar energy for all beings on this planet to live.

All things are connected, the earth, the sun, the sky, the trees, the rivers, the mountains, the birds, the bees, the flowers. All things coexist together. Each individual being is a part of the collective being. This understanding of life is necessary for healing our suffering, the suffering of society, and the suffering occurring on this planet.

In our society, when someone commits a crime, we solve the issue by imprisoning them. We conclude there is no hope for this person and that it is best for them to live in confinement. This will not heal them; it will only produce more suffering.

If we were to look deeply at this person we call a "criminal" we will see that their actions have an underlying cause. We could look into their personal history, how they were raised, how they were treated during their upbringing, how they may have turned to drugs as a way to escape their suffering, and how their suffering caused them to inflict more suffering onto others.

This person does not need to be mistreated and condemned; it is this very behavior that caused them to commit their crime in the first place. They need to be loved, taken care of and healed. They need to receive the treatment they had never been given as a child. When we can see that an individual is a product of the collective, we develop compassion for them.

When someone commits a crime, it is a reflection of the environment they were raised in. We are all responsible for the society that we have produced, as the society is responsible for the individuals that it produces.

Everything has both an individual and collective nature. Only the ego and its illusory way of thinking believe that everything is separate and individual. To touch the reality of who we are, we need to look deeply into nature.

We are all one coexisting entity. When we are identified with the body-mind, we are constantly in search of what will benefit "I," failing to realize that what is best for "I" is what is best for the collective.

The ego likes to think of itself as a separate entity, it wants to find a part of itself that is independent and permanent—one that it can label and define—but such an entity does not exist.

When we fail to realize our collective nature, we are stuck trying to define our individual "self" with thought.

This produces an endless loop of thinking, and eventually we are left with feelings of uncertainty and insecurity, as there is no separate "self" that we can define.

The mind wants to understand itself with thought, but we are not our thoughts; we are the witness of thoughts. We are the awareness within that is eternally present, forever a part of this experience. We are not the ego "I" that thought has created, we are the deeper "I" that precedes thought. This deeper "I" is the source of our being, and it is one with all things.

Like individual waves of the ocean, all experiences arise, live, and dissolve within the ocean of consciousness, the substance and cause of everything. Just as every wave of the ocean is the whole ocean waving, every being in the Universe is the entire Universe being. On the surface, we have this personality, this body, our particular roles in life that we lead—but this is all superficial. Deep down, at the source of our being, we are all connected.

In order for there to be any experience at all, our consciousness must be brought into form. Without forms there would be no stability, no foundation, no ground on which to experience anything other than the formless nature of awareness.

We inhabit these physical forms, and we are experiencing the world of form, though within us, our true nature remains formless and eternal.

It is important not to abandon our individual roles in life, or to become devoid of personality, but it is also important to realize that you are not your roles in life, or your personality. This is all just a game—a dance, an experience, an event, an expression, something to be lived and enjoyed, not something to be suffered and endured. Enjoy this life as your own unique expression of the universe, but realize deep down that you are the universe—you are one with all things. At the very core of existence, all things are connected, all things are a part of the one universal consciousness.

There is not a single being that does not experience themselves as "I." To me, I am "I," and you are "you." But to you, I am "you," and you are "I." Everyone experiences themselves as "I," because they are the center of their experience. This "I"—this deeper awareness—is inherent in all things.

"The soul is the same in all living creatures, although the body of each is different."
— Hippocrates

When you look into the eyes of another being, you are seeing the very same awareness looking back at you. In a sense, you are looking at yourself. There is only one awareness—one consciousness—but it is experiencing itself from an inconceivable amount of perspectives. It is this universal consciousness which creates all things, and animates itself through all things in order to experience and know itself better.

To truly understand the value of something, we have to experience it through contrast. It is because of cold that we truly understand the value of heat. It is because of darkness that we are able to know light. Without sadness, we would not appreciate happiness; and without violence, we would not know the significance of peace.

The consciousness of the universe can only know itself, by experiencing itself from different perspectives. The consciousness that is present in you is the same consciousness that is present in me, every person we know, every animal, insect, mineral, cell, bacteria and particle that exists. Our consciousness is the same omnipresent substance that exists in and as all things, yet all things exist under different conditions and therefor have a different conscious experience based on their unique perspective. (Note that this is only an attempt to put this truth into words, though in no way are words an accurate representation of Truth. The truth of our existence is something that must be discovered personally in order to be known and understood personally. We cannot expect the limited words of language to define the ultimate reality of life).

Although each experience is individual and unique, we are all a part of the collective consciousness of all things. The source of all being is consciousness. If there were no consciousness, how could anything be?

Just as the branches of a tree all come from the same trunk, each individual experience arises from the same source of pure consciousness. And like the branches on the tree, we are different and unique, but not separate.

Each time an individual awakens to their true nature, consciousness is coming to a greater understanding of itself. You are the entire Universe experiencing itself from your unique perspective.

How amazing is it to realize that everything in the universe is an essential part of who you are? That we are all so intimately connected, that there is nothing in this universe that remains alone, and the only reason we ever feel alone is because of our identification with our thoughts and their resistance to accepting our true nature? That all we have to do to be at peace is transcend the illusory thoughts that separate us, realize who we are at our deepest level of being, and connect to the natural source of consciousness within us?

Our purpose here is to experience, live, create, and grow together, all so we can come to a better understanding of who we are—the one universal consciousness. We are not here to fight each other, to work for money, or separate ourselves from the world—this is just an illusion created by the ego.

We have created society and we are responsible for the society that we have created. We have experienced war, oppression, famine, and all kinds of disasters, only to realize the value of peace. We have experienced the contrast of separation, and we know the tragedies that it produces. Now it is time to realize our oneness, and experience the love and peace that this realization produces.

This idea of oneness, of our interconnected existence as the one consciousness of the universe, is not something that I have made up. It is an ancient truth that has been understood throughout history by cultures around the world, and it is the leading edge discovery of quantum physics.

Every culture has a different way of interpreting nature, as language and experience are always relative, but beyond the limitations of language and thought, there exists this profound truth: that we are a part of everyone and everything in existence. Everything is you—or better yet, everything is "I." Of course this is only an attempt to put this experience into words.

Ultimately, language cannot define this profound truth, and thought cannot comprehend it. It is something that can only be felt and experienced right now in this moment.

Stillness

6 A NEW PERSPECTIVE ON RELIGION

Religion is a very touchy subject for most people. But why do you think that is? It seems like people do not have much difficulty speaking openly on many topics, but as soon as you bring up the concept of God, existence, or philosophy, people defensively protect their beliefs and block out any information that may oppose their beloved beliefs.

Whatever someone's belief of God or Life is, it is likely what they base their entire worldview on. Either they live on the foundation that God is their creator, or they are certain of the fact that there is no God. Whatever the case, it seems to be a very touchy subject for most people, and likely one that makes them feel very uncomfortable to discuss.

This sense of discomfort has a root cause; it is born out of uncertainty. If there is any concept or idea that makes us uncomfortable, it means that there is a part of us that doesn't fully understand it, a part of us that is resisting it, a part of us that is preventing us from confronting it, a part of us that is unsure, and likely a part of us that is unconsciously refusing to let us be at peace.

If we really want to be at peace, we need to look into these feelings and understand why they are there. If we do not bring them into our awareness, they will continue to govern us unconsciously.

We only fear things because we don't understand them, because we try to escape them. So to no longer live in fear, we must face our fears. We must come to a greater understanding of the concepts we are afraid to confront.

When I was growing up, there was always a part of me that was irritated by the word "God." I despised hearing people preach about God, or telling me I needed to "find God," and so on. Though I have come to understand that it was not "God" that I was irritated by, it was my misunderstanding of what God was, as well as the word "God" itself which has been distorted throughout history and skewed from its original meaning; so much so that even many ministers and "believers" of God do not really know what it is they are referring to.

Many people share this same sense of irritation when it comes to religion, and their irritation is justified, as mainstream religion has often been misused as a method of controlling the public's perception through fear and religious dogma. But the foundations of religion and their basic spiritual principles still hold tremendous value, and we can benefit greatly by applying some of the core teachings of religion to our experience now.

For the past few centuries, science has attempted to debunk religion and it has allowed us to come to some amazing discoveries. As magnificent as science is, it does have its limitations.

"Science cannot solve the ultimate mystery of nature. And that is because, in the last analysis, we ourselves are a part of the mystery that we are trying to solve."
– Max Planck, Theoretical Physicist

Science has attempted to know nature by dividing it, while spirituality focuses on seeing nature as a whole. The aim of religion and spirituality is to point to the greater reality that exists beyond our ability to know intellectually or explain scientifically. Unfortunately, many people get caught up in the words of religion, and fail to see the greater reality that they are pointing to.

Aristotle—a well-known philosopher of ancient Greece—once said, "It is the mark of an educated man to be able to entertain a thought without accepting it." We too can entertain the idea of something new to us, without accepting it as truth. We do not have to change our opinions or beliefs in order to understand a perspective that differs from ours. To have an open mind, we have to be able to look at reality, without clinging to any thoughts or beliefs about what we think reality is.

There is a message I want to communicate to you that may require you to think of "God" from a different perspective, but you do not have to accept the idea in order to consider it or benefit from it. You can read these words, understand the greater reality that they are pointing to, and apply this understanding to your life however you see fit, without getting caught up in the words or feeling that your beliefs are being attacked.

Our minds always want to know everything, and the message I wish to convey to you is that we simply cannot know everything, as everything we know is only a matter of perspective. Though just because we personally do not know or understand something, does not mean that it doesn't exist, or that we cannot benefit from its existence.

The concept of "God" is something so profound that our minds are incapable of comprehending it in its totality, which is why religion speaks so frequently of "surrendering to God," "Having faith in God," and mentioning that "everything is in God's hands."

There are certain things that exist beyond our control, and "God," the Universe, Consciousness, Nature, The Great Spirit, The Tao, or however you wish to label it, is something that is certainly beyond the control of our thinking mind, since it is the very thing that has produced the thinking mind.

Setting aside any previously held beliefs of what "God" may be, let us, for the time being, come to an agreement that

Stillness

"God" can be defined as "the one universal consciousness of all that exists." God is this universal consciousness, this cosmic energy that organizes, creates and destroys all things. It is the source of being within us, and within all things. It is the very essence of creation and existence, the source of life itself.

We can feel the presence of this cosmic energy within us, but only when the mind is still. When we are lost in thought, overthinking our existence, producing all of this mental noise inside of our heads, we cannot hear the stillness that speaks to us, the inner voice that guides us, and the presence that allows us to feel loved and to be love.

"To understand the immeasurable, the mind must be extraordinarily quiet, still."
— Jiddu Krishnamurti

The mind can only think of the knowledge it has gained from its perspective, it only knows what it has accumulated from its experience. The mind cannot know that which is beyond the mind, and beyond its individual perspective.

In other words, the mind cannot know God. Only this awareness can know God, and can know itself as God. Though this presence of God can only be felt when the mind is silent, when we are in a state of total stillness. Only then can we connect to the source of our being, and when we are connected to our source, we are at peace.

It is only when we drift away from the source that we begin to feel lost, afraid, and confused. When we are rooted in the stillness within us, our mind becomes less controlling, our intuition comes forth, and we have a sense of knowing, a sense of purpose, and a sense of love for life—not just our life, but all life.

This feeling is so profound, and so unexplainable, that it can only be felt. The mind cannot label it, the ego cannot function in it, and nothing but total peace and bliss can be felt in it.

To connect with this feeling yourself, you have to be willing to leave behind the mind and its need to define everything with logic, reason, and thought. You have to surrender your "self" and experience the true nature of God that exists within you.

For the remainder of this chapter, God will represent this cosmic energy within us, the consciousness of the universe that we are all a part of. If you are uncomfortable with that definition, replace it with your own. This definition could apply to Nature, The Universe, The Great Spirit, or anything that refers to all of existence as one unity, but during this chapter I will most often refer to it as "God." But keep in mind that names are not at all important. It is the reality that they point to which is important.

The Limitations of the Mind

The universe is comprised of roughly 96% dark energy (the name that scientists have given to the energy we cannot perceive). This means that everything that is visible to us, everything that we feel, sense, taste, smell, and touch, everything we have observed with all of our scientific instruments, adds up to less than 5% of the total universe.[3]

More than 95% of the universe exists beyond our current perception. This "dark energy"—or the energy our minds cannot perceive—is not something that exists outside of us. It exists within us, through us, and as us.

Human beings only have five senses with which we can perceive our surroundings, six including our extrasensory perception. Would it not be wise to admit that our limited human knowledge could not possibly comprehend the totality of "God," or the one universal consciousness of all that exists?

In the first verse of the *Tao Te Ching*, an ancient Taoist text, Lao Tzu says:

---

[3] http://www.space.com/11642-dark-matter-dark-energy-4-percent-universe-panek.html

"The Tao that can be told is not the eternal Tao.
The name that can be named is not the eternal Name."

Tao or Name being what we are referring to as God in this chapter, the God that can be defined or explained is not the eternal God. The totality of God exists beyond our comprehension.

The verse continues:

"The unnamable is the eternally real.
Naming is the origin of all particular things.
Free from desire, you realize the mystery. Caught in
desire, you see only the manifestations. Yet mystery
and manifestations arise from the same source. This
source is called darkness. Darkness within darkness.
The gateway to all understanding."

This source of darkness that Lao Tzu is referring to, is called darkness because we cannot perceive it. We could even propose that he is speaking of this dark energy which makes up 95% of the universe.

"Darkness within darkness, the gateway to all understanding," implies that in order for us to understand, we have to remain in the darkness of not knowing: "darkness within darkness." In other words, to truly understand, we have to accept that we simply cannot understand. As paradoxical as this concept may seem, it will become clearer to you as you read further in this chapter.

We are only able to perceive that which is perceptible by our six sense organs (eyes, ears, nose, tongue, body, and mind). The things that we sense are limited to the organs with which we can sense them.

Take sound for example: sound waves exist as variations of pressure in a medium such as air. They are created by the vibration of an object, which causes the air surrounding the object to vibrate. The vibrating air then causes the eardrum to vibrate, which the brain interprets as sound.

So the answer to the old question: If a tree falls in the woods and no one is around to hear it, does it make a sound? is actually no. It will make a vibration, but without an eardrum and brain to interpret that vibration, it will not exist as sound.

Our sense organs just pick up vibrations from the universe around us, then send signals to our brains, which then interprets these signals to form a perception of our surroundings. We only have six sense organs; we are not able to perceive the innumerable vibrations that exist beyond our abilities to perceive them.

Some animals demonstrate clearly the difference of our abilities to sense distinctive frequencies. Whales, dolphins, and bats for example use echolocation—their biological sonar—as a way to perceive their surroundings. Echolocation enables animals to emit a high frequency sound out to the environment and listen to the echoes of that sound that return from various objects near them. They use these echoes to locate and identify the objects for means of navigation or foraging.

The sounds emitted by these animals have such a high frequency, that they are unable to be detected by the human eardrum. This is just one example, but again it demonstrates clearly that we are not able to perceive everything that is happening around us.

There is no way that our minds could perceive the billions of different energies flowing through and around our being. Because of our limited perception, our understanding of "God" or the Universe is also limited. Our minds couldn't possibly grasp the totality of "God" with our restricted perspective, nor could we define it within the limitations of human language and thought.

God is something that exists within us, yet it is still beyond the boundary of sensory perceptions and feelings. It is the consciousness that precedes perception and feeling; the awareness in which sensory perception and feeling occur. It is not something that we can reach; it is something we already are—the very essence of life itself.

Our attempt to know nature in its totality is ultimately futile, as is our attempt to view ourselves as something that exists separately from nature. Our perception is always limited to our individual experience and the way that our minds are conditioned to perceive.

The scientist attempts to know nature in one way, and from his perspective he is right. The religious man attempts to know nature a different way, but from his perspective he is also right. It is the same nature that they are attempting to know, but their interpretations of nature vary. It does not mean that one is more or less true than the other, it just means that their perspectives of nature are limited to their experiences. It is impossible to know nature because that which we perceive to be nature, is only the idea of nature according to each person's mind.

Those who think they know God couldn't possibly know God, since their understanding of the Universe is limited to their accumulated knowledge of it. Those that admit they do not and cannot know God have an actual understanding of what God is—it is the total reality of nature that exists beyond our limited perception.

This is explained in the Hindu Upanishads, one of the oldest religious texts known to exist:

"He who thinks that God is not comprehended, by him God is comprehended; But he who thinks that God is comprehended knows him not. God is unknown to those who know him, and is known to those who do not know him at all."
— *Upanishads*

There is no correct view of the Universe, and no way we could know the totality of all that exists with our limited perspectives of life. Every perspective of nature is unique to each individual. Even conclusions based on piles of data are analyzed and interpreted individually. No two perspectives are alike. The true nature of the universe is unknowable.

"The world itself is a unity of matter within the flow of experience, but people's minds divide phenomena into dualities such as life and death, light and dark, love and hate, etc. The mind begins to believe that what the senses perceive is the absolute truth. The forms of the material world, concepts of life and death, light and dark, love and hate, all originate within the mind.

People think they understand things because they become familiar with them, though this is superficial knowledge. It is the astronomer who knows the name of stars, the botanist who knows the classifications of leaves and flowers, the artist who knows the aesthetics of green and red, but this is not to know nature itself.

The astronomer, botanist, and artist have done no more than grasp impressions and interpret them, each within the vault of their own mind. By discriminating phenomena, we fragment and observe individual parts, forming an incomplete understanding of the natural world. There is no definite answer to the question of existence that we are capable of understanding. It seems that the best way for us to know nature is by admitting that we know nothing."

— Masanobu Fukuoka

The Perception Reflection

Everything we know about the universe is only our perception of it. It is the accumulated knowledge of names, labels, judgments, opinions, discriminations, etc. Yet nature itself remains unnamable, without labels, judgments, opinions, or discriminations.

Thoughts are a result of our knowledge; they come from what is known to our brains. Everything you think is thought in a language that is known to you—words, images, concepts, ideas, and so on. With our thoughts we make the world what it is to us, but without our thoughts the world remains unmade. With our thoughts we name the world, but without our thoughts the world remains nameless.

Gautama Buddha also recognized this truth. The *Dhamapadda* (a collection of the Buddha's teachings) mentions that our perception of the world is what the world is to us:

> *"All that we are is the result of what we have thought: it is founded on our thoughts and made up of our thoughts. If a man speaks or acts with an evil thought, suffering follows him as the wheel follows the hoof of the beast that draws the wagon.... If a man speaks or acts with a good thought, happiness follows him like a shadow that never leaves him."*
> — *Gautama Buddha*

The true reality of Nature, or shall we say "God," is unknowable, unnamable, and eternal. It remains so, and how we interpret this unknowable reality, is how we will experience it. "All we are is the result of what we have thought." The reality we experience is a reflection of our perception.

So whether we perceive the world to be a dangerous, hostile and negative place, or we perceive it as a beautiful, loving and peaceful place, we are correct. Our consciousness has the power to create our individual reality, and our individual realities create the collective reality.

The world exists according to how we think it exists. How we perceive the Universe, how we perceive each other, and how we perceive ourselves makes all the difference.

Everything in society was first created by thought. If we were to think harmonious thoughts, followed by harmonious actions, the world would be a peaceful place. The state of the world is a reflection of our state of being. Peace starts from within.

A New Perspective on Religion

In the Christian Bible it states:

*"In the beginning was the Word, and the Word was
with God, and the Word was God."*
— John 1:1

*"Through him (the Word) all things were made;
without him, nothing was made that has been made."*
— John 1:3

Could this not be another way of saying that the Word
is what creates our world, and without the Word our world
remains uncreated? That our language has named what we
call "the world," but without our language it remains
unnamed? That all that we perceive to be the world is
nothing but our perception of it? That "the world" is what
we have created, but God remains the creator?

I am not at all trying to discredit religion, but I do firmly
believe that most religions have been mistranslated over the
years and skewed from their original meanings, to the extent
that most people do not know what they are referring to
when they speak of God, or Eternal Life.

Seeing God in this light—as cosmic energy or the
universal consciousness of all that exists—still implies that
God is our creator, since it is this cosmic energy from which
we were born, what we exist as now, and in death to which
we shall return.

God is not a being in the sky above us that watches our
every step. God is not confined to a form. God is
formless—it is the essence of life itself flowing through us,
and existing as us. If consciousness was something that was
created by an outside God, it still wouldn't make a
difference whether our minds could grasp where it came
from, what existed before it, or what created it; it would be
more important to dwell on the simple fact that it exists. It
exists and we are responsible for how we use it now, in this
moment.

If someone or something did create the consciousness of the Universe, it would still have to have a consciousness of its own, as would whatever made that consciousness, and that consciousness's consciousness, and so on and so on. Consciousness is not the creation; it is the creator—the very source of creation itself.

This theory of "creation" is not an attempt to discredit the scientific theory of evolution either, but rather a realization that creation and evolution are just two sides of the same coin.

Each fragment of the universal consciousness is creating its individual reality, as well as being created by its collective reality, and as this happens on a mass scale, the universal consciousness continually evolves.

Our individual realities are creating our collective reality, just as the collective reality is also creating our individual reality. Each cell is reacting to its environment as well as creating its environment. Each person is doing the same. The individual and the collective are not separate.

The problem that most people have with accepting, let alone even considering this theory, is that it is so vast and comprehensive that it is beyond the ability to be fully understood by our limited minds and fragmented perspectives—it is beyond the ego—and if we are to ever have lasting peace in our lives, we have to let go of the ego's need for control and the mind's desire to know everything, and surrender to "God" or the natural flow of the Universe. We must give up our imagined control and allow it to be returned to Nature. We have to stop trying to figure out the world and simply start experiencing the world. We must allow our own essential nature to flow freely through us.

"Life is not a puzzle to be solved, but a mystery
to be lived."
— Alan Watts

Surrendering to God

In almost every religious tradition, they speak of surrendering to God, or having faith in God. Many people equate Faith with Belief, but the two are actually very different.

Beliefs are ideas that we cling to as a foundation for how we view the world—something we use to make sense of our reality. Beliefs are nothing but our strong opinions about life—something created during the course of our development and past experiences.

Faith, on the other hand, does not require holding onto any ideas or concepts; it requires the opposite. To have faith in something requires letting go of our imagined control and trusting the course that Nature will take. So to have faith in God is to trust the natural course of the universe—something that we inevitably have no control over anyway.

"The attitude of faith is to let go, and become open to truth, whatever it might turn out to be."
– Alan Watts

Christians say that one must surrender oneself in order to receive the love of God. Is this not another way to say that one must give up one's identification with the ego—the idea of a separately existing self—in order to feel the loving connection that they feel when they realize their true nature as God (the one universal consciousness of all that exists)?

Taoists believe that they must have faith in the Tao, meaning they must give up the idea of "I" having any control over Nature, and must allow Nature to take its course.

The examples are limitless, and we can apply this understanding of God to nearly any religion. To say that we must surrender ourselves to God, is to say that we must give up our idea of being an independently existing self (ego), and embrace the truth that we are all a part of everything in existence; and that once we realize this, we can receive the love of God, which is simply the profound sensation that we experience when we realize our true existence as the one awareness of the universe—a realization that many people refer to as "enlightenment."

So how do we realize our true existence as awareness? How do we give up the feeling of being separate from nature—of feeling like an "I" existing apart from the world, rather than existing as the world?

We have to understand that we have always been awareness. No matter what happens it is always happening within the field of consciousness. This consciousness is who we really are. When we are identified with the body, the mind, or the ego, we fail to see that we are the awareness in which the body, mind, and ego exist, and so we suffer when things happen to the body, mind, or ego, because we believe these things are actually happening to us.

Your suffering is not really yours, it belongs to your ego, and you are not your ego. We have to learn to stop identifying with these things that are not us. We are not our body; we merely exist within a body. We can use this body to experience the world and achieve things in the world, but we are not the body.

We have to be willing to give up our accumulated knowledge of what we think the world is, and experience the present moment, without trying to understand it, explain it, judge it, criticize it, compare it to what we know, or see it as something happening apart from ourselves.

We have to realize that it is impossible to define life. Everything we attempt to define as life is limited to our perception of life, not to mention that it is constantly changing. We need to stop attempting to label this experience, and simply experience reality openly, having no fixed idea of what it is that we are experiencing. We must be totally and fully aware, completely attentive of the present moment, having no thought of an "I" that is trying to make sense of the experience.

A New Perspective on Religion

*"Seek not the law in your scriptures, for the law is life,
whereas the scripture is dead.*

*I tell you truly, Moses received not his laws from God
in writing, but through the living word.*

*The law is living word of living God to living prophets
for living men.*

*In everything that is life is the law written. You find it
in the grass, in the tree, in the river, in the mountain, in
the birds of heaven, in the fishes of the sea; but seek it
chiefly in yourselves.*

*For I tell you truly, all living things are nearer to God
than the scripture, which is without life.*

*God so made life and all living things that they might by
the everlasting word teach the laws of the true God to
man. God wrote not the laws in the pages of books, but
in your heart and in your spirit. They are in your breath,
your blood, your bone; in your flesh, your bowels, your
eyes, your ears, and in every little part of your body.*

*They are present in the air, in the water, in the
earth, in the plants, in the sunbeams, in the depths
and in the heights.*

*They all speak to you that you may understand the
tongue and the will of the living God.*

*But you shut your eyes that you may not see, and you
shut your ears that you may not hear.*

*I tell you truly, that the scripture is the work of man,
but life and all its hosts are the work of our God.
Wherefore do you not listen to the words of God which
are written in His works?*

*And wherefore do you study the dead scriptures which
are the work of the hands of men?"*

*– From the words of Jesus Christ, documented in the
Dead Sea Scrolls, (Essene Gospel of Peace: Book 1)*

God is the ever present reality that exists beyond the
limited knowledge of our thinking mind. The only way we
can know God is by leaving behind all of our knowledge of
what we think God is. To have a belief or mental image of
what God is, and to look only for a God that matches that
belief, is to close ourselves off from any real understanding
of what God may be.

The reason that most religious traditions speak of having
faith in God, is because they know that God is unknowable
by means of intellectual knowledge or conceptualization,
and so we must surrender our egos—our mental images of
"I" —in order to truly understand what God is, and to
experience God as God exists in each moment. We must
stop interrupting our experience of life with a constant
stream of thoughts.

Our thoughts cannot understand "God" for as long as
we are thinking; our experience is our thoughts, and it is not
the experience of life in the present moment. The present
moment is just as indefinable as God, and to experience the
present moment without judging it, is to experience God as
God really exists.

*"Zen master is not trying to give you ideas about life;
he is trying to give you life itself, to make you realize
life in and around you, to make you live it instead of
being a mere spectator...A symphony is not explained
by a mathematical analysis of its notes; the mystery of
a woman's beauty is not revealed by a postmortem
dissection; and no one ever understood the wonder of a
bird on the wing by stuffing it and putting it in a glass
case. To understand these things, you must live and*

move with them as they are alive. The same is true of the universe: no amount of intellectual analysis will explain it, for philosophy and science can only reveal its mechanism, never its meaning or, as the Chinese say, its Tao.

"What is the Tao?" A Zen master answers, "Usual life is the very Tao." "How does one bring oneself into accord with it?" "If you try to accord with it, you will get away from it." For to imagine that there is a "you" separate from life which somehow has to accord with life is to fall straight into the trap... Self-consciousness is a stoppage because it is like interrupting a song after every note so as to listen to the echo, and then feeling irritated because of the loss of rhythm."
– Alan Watts

Stillness

7 LIFE IN THE MOMENT

When we are fully embraced in our experience, we are naturally quite joyful. As soon as we separate ourselves from the moment with our thoughts, our joy is taken away. Can you recall a moment when you were totally interested and absorbed in your experience, doing something that required your complete attention, like participating in an intense sport, performing an intricate dance, or watching an interesting film?

When our attention is focused on the moment, we have no consciousness of "self." We are not thinking of "I," or what the purpose of life is, who we are, or what needs to be done, we are just totally absorbed in the experience of the present moment.

We don't see ourselves as something separate from this moment; we are this moment. The only time we feel a sense of separation is when we think of ourselves as an "I" experiencing the moment.

If the thought of "I" is something that exists only when our attention is taken away from the present moment, then we can see how the ego—or the mental image of a separate "I"—is just a result of our mind's way of thinking, and not something that exists in reality.

Our self-consciousness and anxiety are produced by our addiction to thought, and our refusal to silence our mind and bring our awareness back into this moment. These feelings occur only when we think about ourselves experiencing the moment, rather than just experiencing the moment without any thought of a separate "self."

How many people do you think have suffered from nervousness or stage fright because as soon as they were the center of attention, they began to think about themselves, rather than being focused on the experience at hand?

Most people, including myself, are guilty of experiencing this at least once in our lives. We think about ourselves and how we should act or what we should say and suddenly we have no clue of either. Only when we are absorbed in our experience do we feel free to just be.

Eternal Life

Each of us has a passion and purpose unique to us, something that we are to provide for the greater whole of life. If we listen to the voice within us, we will know what this purpose is. It is the thing that gives us the most joy, the thing that makes us feel inspired, and the thing that we feel we can provide to serve and benefit others. Though rather than following our passion and our purpose, most people suppress their natural wisdom; they let the voices of others drown out their inner voice and they live a life that is not in harmony with the life they are meant to live.

The conditioned mind—the mind programmed by society—has influenced us to live according to how others think we should live. If we still the mind, we can feel within us the instinctual drive of how to live, how to be, and how to thrive in each moment of our experience.

We have to learn how to listen to this wisdom inherent within us, so that we may allow it to guide us through life. We have to learn to follow our intuition, and not the skeptical and careful mind conditioned by fear and scarcity.

When we stop thinking about life and start feeling it, experiencing it, and living it, everything changes. We are no longer focused on ourselves and our own personal drama, we are just focused on the present moment, and existing in harmony with all of the things happening in this moment.

We begin to see ourselves as a part of all that exists, realizing and understanding the importance of our unique existence. We see that we are not confined to the idea of "me" and all of its problems, but that we are an integral part of the greater whole, and that our very existence is providing its unique purpose for all of Life.

By surrendering our "self" to Nature, we are giving up our idea of existing apart from Nature and we begin existing as Nature in each moment. This is the meaning of eternal life. Life in the eternity of now.

To live in this way – to experience eternal life – we have to be aware of each moment, feeling it, experiencing it, in touch with it—without our thoughts separating us from it. We must be so fully interested in each moment that thoughts of our "self" do not exist because we are completely absorbed in the now.

When living in this way, we are not conscious of our existence as "me." All we know is our experience at this moment, and it is this experience of consciousness in the moment, that is the only true self that exists, and it is one with all things.

If you want to be happy, live now, in this moment. See each moment as a new experience, don't compare it to the experiences of the past. Forgive the past, accept the past, and let go of your emotional hold on the past.

Leaving behind all of our knowledge of what life is, letting go of our beliefs, and surrendering ourselves and our attention to the present moment, without trying to define it, compare it, judge it, criticize it, or understand it—this is how we awaken to the true reality of life. This is how we experience the present moment and realize that we are the present moment. This is how we feel our

oneness and our connection to all things. This is how we
receive the love of God.

8 THE SPIRIT OF LOVE

Love is our natural state of being. It is the sensation we feel when we realize our connection with Nature—when we see ourselves in another person, and understand that that person is us. The love we feel for our parents, our children, our friends, our family, or our partner, is the same love—the only difference is the appropriate way to express that love with each individual.

"To love is to recognize yourself in another."
– Eckhart Tolle

If we love another person, it is because we feel connected to that person, we have compassion for them, we understand them, and we realize that we are one with them. Though we are always connected to everyone and everything, we do not need another to express their love in order for us to feel the sensation of Love.

In fact, some of the most profound feelings of Love that we can experience occur when we look within ourselves and realize our connection with all things. Sitting where you are right now, you too can feel your connection to everything. You can feel the Spirit of Life within you and the feeling of Love that this connection provides.

All you have to do is silence your mind, take a deep breath, feel the love in your heart, and exhale a smile of joy. Feel deeply your inseparable nature with all of existence, and be grateful for the experience that it provides you with.

Try to hold your breath for as long as you possibly can; the next time you gasp for air; I guarantee you will see clearly how you are that air, and that air is you. Then you can smile to that breath of air and be grateful for the opportunity of life that it allows you to experience.

Try to go a whole day without eating food or drinking water; the next time you eat or drink you will more than likely understand that you are that food and water, and that food and water is you. Then you can smile to that food and water and appreciate it fully.

Even your thoughts, language, ideas, beliefs, etc., were produced by the influence of society and culture. Society is you, and you are society.

"All things share the same breath – the beast, the tree, the man – the air shares its spirit with all the life it supports."
– Chief Seattle

Seeing things from this perspective, we understand that we are the Universe and everything in it. There is no ego, no separate existing "I." All things exist together. The individual is within the collective, just as the collective is within the individual.

The ego is only produced by our thoughts and their eagerness to find permanence in a Universe that is always changing. It is because of our failure to see our oneness with existence that the ego is produced. It is born out of fear, which is an illusion created by a lack of understanding.

Spirit on the other hand, always exists. We are always

connected to everything in the Universe. Though when we perceive our experience as the ego, we are unaware of our connection as Spirit and we don't feel the Love that this connection provides.

In order to feel the Love of God, we must surrender ourselves. In order to feel our connection with Nature, we must give up the idea of a separate existing self (ego).

When the mind is polluted with thought, the noise drowns out the silence within us, the loving presence that can only be felt in a state of stillness.

Our true nature is Love and we are ultimately inseparable from Love, we just have to be willing to throw out the idea of being an "I" that exists apart from the world. The idea of a separate "I" is an illusion produced by fear, and it is the only reason we ever feel any separation from our loving connection to all things.

With this understanding, we can see how the ego, out of fear, attaches itself to other things. It is the ego that clings to the world because it fails to realize that it is the world. Failure to understand this is what has produced our great misconception of what Love is.

Fear and Love

Many people confuse love with attachment, which is a quality of fear—the fear of loss—and it results in insecurity and dependency, which has been the cause of many broken hearts and failed relationships.

The qualities of Fear are attachment, dependency, and resistance. The qualities of Love are appreciation, understanding, and acceptance. We can observe very easily in our personal relationships whether we are acting out of Fear or Love.

Looking at an intimate relationship with a partner for example, if we are selfish, clingy, jealous, spiteful, mistrusting, dependent, etc., our relationship is composed primarily of Fear or ego. If, however we are selfless, understanding, accepting, appreciative, caring, supporting and trusting, our relationship is composed primarily of Love or Spirit.

It is possible to feel both Love and Fear as we fluctuate from the understanding of oneness to the illusory perception of existing as a separate self. Our society is supportive of the ego, so it is easy to be influenced into a state of fear and separation while on the path of realizing our oneness.

All emotions are essentially produced by feelings of either Fear or Love; either seeing ourselves as the ego—separate, or understanding our existence as spirit—connected. Fear and our idea of separation produce feelings of attachment, resistance, anxiety, anger, violence, hatred, jealousy, envy, depression, etc. Love and our understanding of oneness produce feelings of freedom, acceptance, security, calmness, peace, understanding, gratitude, trust, compassion, happiness, etc.

Love is energy; it is powerful, accepting, and immense. Love is the energy that we need to embrace in order to heal our society, our planet, and ourselves.

Learn to love all beings, especially those that hurt you or cause you pain, as they are the ones that need love the most.

Love is often seen as a trait of the weak, though this is far from the truth. To be loving in a world controlled by fear is an act of courage, not weakness.

Many men are raised with the attitude of toughness, that they need to "man up," "act like a man," etc. They are taught not to feel their emotions and as a result, they become very coldhearted.

Acting in this way does not take strength; it is a weak quality, and an attempt to escape and neglect your emotions rather than feel them. It takes real strength to be able to acknowledge your feelings, to feel your emotions and to forgive a situation. Love is a quality of the strong, not the weak.

The Spirit of Love

"Darkness cannot drive out darkness;
only light can do that.
Hate cannot drive out hate;
only love can do that."
– Martin Luther King, Jr.

This powerful Loving energy exists within us all, but it is a connection you have to feel with your heart, not something you can think with your brain. As we have discussed already, there are certain things that cannot be truly comprehended by the intellectual mind.

We are capable of feeling Love and the emotions that it produces, while not having to know why or think about their relation to "I." Putting a requirement on love only limits the amount of love you are capable of feeling.

To experience unconditional love—love without conditions—we have to be willing to leave behind our thoughts and our minds' need to label every experience. We have to take a leap into the unknown and realize that life is happening now, and can only be experienced now.

Our tendency to resist the now and dwell in the familiarity of our thoughts is the cause of our suffering. We have become so addicted to thought that we have identified ourselves with our thoughts and our fear of the unknown, and in doing so we have lost the connection to our true selves and no longer feel the loving sensation that this feeling provides.

To be at peace, we have to return our awareness to the present moment, which we can do at any time and any place. We cannot live happily when we are separated from the moment, lost in the repetitive anxiety of our thinking mind.

Before we discuss exactly how to live life peacefully in the present moment, we have to realize clearly how resistance to the moment is the cause of our suffering. If we can understand our suffering, we can see plainly that we are the cause of it, and we can then work on healing our conditioned way of thinking, in order to live a life of peace.

Stillness

9 RESISTANCE

The present moment is constantly dying, and constantly being reborn. It is always changing, and always new. The moment we try to think about it or understand it, it has already passed, already died, and already been reborn into a new moment. One can see how trying to cling to the present moment is like trying to catch air—it always eludes our grasp.

When we cling to moments in time, it is like holding a hot coal. The longer we hold on, the more pain we feel. The moment we let go, we feel relief. Clinging to the past will always make us feel pain, because resistance to accepting things as they are now is what creates our pain.

The reason that resisting the moment creates the experience of pain is because resistance is caused by seeing ourselves as something that exists apart from our experience. The sense of "I" trying to escape pain is what creates more pain, just as the feeling of "I" trying to escape fear evokes the experience of fear.

As soon as we give up the idea that we exist apart from experience and stop trying to escape it, we no longer feel the feelings of pain or fear that are produced from the idea of a separate "I" trying to escape the moment.

When we are afraid of something, we are resisting it.

But as soon as we face our fear what happens? The fear usually ceases; it was caused solely by our resistance.

Sadness exists in the same manner. We are sad because we are resisting the moment now by clinging to a moment in the past. When we try to compare our experience with our memory, we don't understand the moment as deeply as we do when we are aware of it without comparison.

When we are sad or afraid, we want to escape the moment and avoid the experience. Our only escape is into our memory, into what is known, and so we think of how things were then, and how they are now, and the self-pity of a separate existing "I" is produced.

We feel safe dwelling in our memory because it is fixed and known, but it no longer exists and therefore it is dead. It is not the moment now, which is unknown and living. The idea of "I" existing apart from the moment is only an illusion. The pain is inescapable and resisting it only makes it worse.

"People have a hard time letting go of their suffering. Out of a fear of the unknown, they prefer suffering that is familiar."
— Thich Nhat Hanh

Too often we try to label our experience, to resist it by seeing it as something that a separate "I" is experiencing, rather than just seeing it as who we are in the moment. When we are sad, we say, "I am sad." Though "sad" is just a word, we are not that word. The thing we attempt to define as "sad" is an energy, a feeling, an emotion. It is our reality in the present moment and to understand our sadness, we must be willing to experience it. We cannot be free of our sadness by trying to escape it or by labeling it or giving it a name. We have to feel into it, accept it, and understand what caused it, why it is present, and how we can restore our peace.

If we refrain from trying to escape pain and accept that

we cannot escape our experience, what happens? We are forced to deal with the experience at hand and feel the pain. But once we do this—once we actually stop trying to escape pain and feel this pain—we see that the experience of pain almost completely ceases, it was caused by our resistance to being aware of our feelings in the present moment.

Fighting pain is pain, trying to escape fear is fear. As long as we are unaware that our experience is us, we will try to escape it as a separate "I." When we face the fact that we are our experience and we feel the pain and fear and go into it, it usually begins to cease, or at least becomes much more tolerable. But so long as "I" is resisting the moment, pain and suffering will always be produced.

Stillness

10 THE CAUSE OF SUFFERING

The only reason that anyone suffers is because of their resistance to the present moment. In other words, our thoughts are responsible for our suffering.

Physical pain is different from suffering or emotional pain. We may feel physical pain, but it does not necessarily result in our suffering. Our suffering is produced by our resistance to Life.

Everything in the Universe is constantly changing. When we resist this change—when we cling to the things that are changing or expect them to change differently—we suffer. Our suffering is caused by attachment—by holding onto people, objects, ideas, images, desires, or thoughts—and resisting the reality of how things exist now, in the present moment.

In order for there to be attachment, you need two things: the person or thing being attached to, and the person who's attaching. In other words, "attachment" requires seeing the object of attachment as being separate from oneself. Seeing oneself and everything else in this way is a delusion. Further, it is a delusion that is the deepest cause of our unhappiness. It is caused by mistakenly seeing ourselves as separate from everything else to which we "attach."

Because we think we have intrinsic existence within our

skin, and what's outside our skin is "everything else," we go through life grabbing for one thing after another to make us feel safe, or to make us happy. We "pursue" happiness because we think it comes from outside of ourselves. But it's also because we think things are outside of ourselves that we are stressed about them and worry about them

How many times have you caused your own suffering by wanting things to be different than the way they are? How many times have you suffered because you were too afraid of change, too attached to a person, relationship, or object? How many times has your reluctance to accept things as they are resulted in your own suffering? Be honest with yourself.

If we look back, we will realize that the only time we ever suffer is when we resist the way that things are—when we desire for a situation to be different. Our suffering is caused by our refusal to live in the present moment, and our attachment to things that are impermanent, mainly our memories of the past or expectations of the future. We wish for impermanent things to remain permanent, and once they begin to change, as all things inevitably do, we suffer because of our unwillingness to let go of our attachments.

It is difficult to get over the loss of someone you love, the end of a long relationship, or a sudden change in your usual routine—but there is a time to grieve, in which we feel deeply these feelings of grief and let them all out—and a time to stop resisting the moment, to stop clinging to how things were, and to let go and accept how things are now.

If we do not give ourselves time to feel our emotions, they will be repressed and they will begin to control our experience subconsciously. We have to accept them, feel them, and release them so that we can be free of them.

It will also bring us peace to remember that although one form has come to an end, as all eventually do, they are still a part of the formless nature of the Universe. They are still with you—in your heart, your memory, the ways they affected the world—and they will always be a part of the

74

greater reality which is you, the collective consciousness of all that exists. Their physical form may have changed, but their energy lives on. Energy is neither created nor destroyed—it only transfers from one form to another.

Clinging to certain forms, whether they be physical or mental, will always lead to suffering, and the only way to be free of this suffering is to accept the new reality, silence our thoughts, and bring our awareness back into the experience of the present moment.

> *"People give rise to feelings of hatred and love for these objects of the six senses, and because of this subjectivity they accumulate countless knots of habits that cover up their Buddha-nature (true nature). Even if they labor at various practices, as long as they have not gotten rid of the defilement in their minds, there is no way they can be liberated. When you look into the root basis, it is all due to fixating the mind on form."*
> *– Hui-Neng*

In Zen, it is said that all things are essentially empty (formless). By this it means that there is no "thing" which exists in and of itself. All things exist because of all other things. A flower only exists because of the things that are not a "flower"—the soil, the compost, the air, the rain, and the sun. The true nature of the "flower" is empty.

The mind likes to cling to things that it knows—the knowledge it has accumulated from its experiences—but it is this accumulated knowledge that makes the mind. The true nature of the mind is also empty.

When we do not realize the formless nature of all things, we cling to forms, and when these forms change as all forms inevitably do, we suffer because of our attachments to them.

All attachments are produced by our thoughts, which are incapable of grasping the concept of formlessness. To understand clearly the formless nature of things, we have to let go of our attachment to thought, and experience reality as it exists in this moment.

We hardly ever allow ourselves to just be in the present moment. Our time and attention are wasted on our thoughts, anticipating the future, or clinging to the past.

If you suffer from anxiety, tension, unease, stress, or worry it is because you are too focused on the future. If you suffer from guilt, regret, grievance, sadness, depression, hatred, or bitterness, it is because you are too attached to the past. When your attention is fully focused on being aware in the present moment, you experience peace.

> *"The future is a concept—it doesn't exist. There is*
> *no such thing as tomorrow. There never will be*
> *because time is always now. That's one of the things*
> *we discover when we stop talking to ourselves and*
> *stop thinking. We find there is only present, only an*
> *eternal now."*
> *– Alan W. Watts*

We suffer when we are not here and now, aware of the moment in the moment, adapting to change and welcoming it with an open heart. Take a deep breath, silence your thoughts, and relax. If you are able to do this, you will see that nothing is lacking in the present moment.

If you just thought of something that is lacking, it was not the present moment, but your thoughts about it that produced your feeling of lack. Rather than being in the moment, most people try to analyze the moment and think about what the moment means. Your thoughts can never understand the significance of the present moment, for as soon as you think a thought about it, the moment has already passed.

Everything you have read so far in this book is now something in the past. Even the sentence that just told you so. Change is the only constant, and if you are fully present, aware of the moment, you can flow with the change and be one with it. The only way to experience the present moment is to be fully aware, fully present, here and now.

If our thoughts create our reality and are able to produce our suffering, it would make sense that we take some time and personal involvement in the process of being aware of our thoughts and conditioning ourselves to think in a harmonious way.

Our state of mind is naturally clear. It is only when thoughts begin to cloud our minds that we no longer experience peace. If we are able to detach from our thoughts and return to the natural state of awareness that is our true nature, we can find peace in our daily lives and be content with our experience.

"Detachment is not that you should own nothing, but that nothing should own you."
– Ali Ibn Abi Talib

Just as our minds were empty, open, and aware as infants, so too must our minds be empty, open, and aware if we are to experience the present moment. We must return our minds to the natural state that existed before any thoughts were imprinted upon them.

Our natural state is peace. Only when we add things to our natural state do we become upset, discontent, sad, angry, depressed, and all of the other emotions. If we can let go of all these emotions, what will remain is peace.

When we have nothing, we are peaceful. Some may disagree with that and even be sad at the thought of "having nothing," which is understandable since we have been conditioned to think that way, but understand it is not "nothing" that makes you sad, it is just the thought and the attachment to possessions that create such emotions. It is the thought of losing "something" that creates sadness, not the idea of having "nothing."

If the thought of "nothing" makes you sad, it is because your mind is still clinging to "something." When we are sad it is because we have "something" to be sad about. When we are mad it is because we have "something" to be angry about. When we are afraid it is because we have "something" to fear. But if we can allow ourselves to release these thoughts that weigh us down, and can let go of our beliefs and our way of thinking, we will see that there is "nothing" to worry about, "nothing" to fear, "nothing" to upset us, and "nothing" to make us sad.

If we are not attached to "something" we are left with "nothing" and there is no longer anything weighing us down or preventing us from feeling free and at ease in the present moment.

Only our thoughts, attachments, and resistance to being in the present moment make us suffer, but within us is always a state of peace.

We all have things that happen in our experience, things that may upset us, make us stress, or feel depressed. But the longer you hold onto these things, the heavier they get.

You can hold onto a ten-pound weight with little difficulty, but if you try to hold that weight for hours, your arms will strain, get tense, and feel weak. The psychological weight that we carry is no different. We can think about our loss, our memories of the past, our worries about the future, and they will not cause us much suffering. But the longer we dwell on these thoughts, the heavier they get, and the more stressed, tensed, and weak we feel.

We can be at peace any time we want to be. We just have to let go of all the things that weigh us down. We have to accept the reality now and release the psychological weights that we are carrying.

The more you let go, and the less you try to control or worry, the lighter you feel. You begin to realize that there is absolutely "nothing" preventing you from being at peace except for your own negative thoughts and attachments.

Only when we allow the things outside of us to take over the natural state of peace within us, do we begin to suffer. But all of this can be healed simply by changing our thoughts and letting go of the things that we cling to.

"You need nothing to be happy,
but you need something to be sad."
— Mooji

The Pleasure-Pain Principle

There is a concept familiar to many philosophers and psychologists known as "the pleasure-pain principle." The pleasure principle mentions that we are born seeking an immediate gratification of needs, for which our bodies reward us with feelings of pleasure. The pain principle says that, whilst seeking pleasure people will also seek to avoid pain, inevitably causing pain so long as they are resisting pain and receiving no immediate experiences of pleasure.

The pleasure-pain principle is a repetitive cycle in which one seeking fulfillment from pleasure is inevitably left with the experience of pain. The ego seeks selfishly for gratification and stimulation of the senses because it distracts our awareness from the present moment. But so long as the ego is avoiding the present moment, it will always produce its own suffering.

When we are experiencing something pleasurable, we are fully immersed in that experience, but because we do not entirely understand experience or the reality of the present moment, we cling to that experience, and as soon as the experience ends the ego is left alone to face the reality of the present moment. Feelings of fear and the thoughts of being separate from the moment then return, and the ego once again seeks to continually find more pleasure and more satisfaction in order to escape this painful feeling, resulting in further pain as the ego does not receive the pleasure it desires.

Desire is a form of resistance that is perhaps the most destructive. So much suffering is caused by our desires. The modern human lives in a constant state of desire, always wanting what they don't have, never satisfied with life as it is.

We want money, material items, nice cars, big houses; we want to travel around the world, find a life partner, become successful. There is nothing wrong with any of these things, in themselves; but they become destructive when the idea of attaining them takes us away from being content with our life in the present moment.

We think that we won't be happy until we have the thing that we desire, failing to see that it is this desire that is making us unhappy. People will go through so many difficulties just to fulfill their desires. But what happens when we get what we are seeking? What happens when we finally get that car we've wanted, those clothes we longed for, or that experience we craved? We are usually only satisfied with these things for a small amount of time, and then, its off to the next desire.

Looking for happiness in external objects will never bring us peace. Our lack of peace is produced by a lack of understanding our true nature. Happiness exists within us, and will only come to us when we become grateful for what we have, and content with the life we live. It will not come by resisting the moment and seeking for a new moment, but by facing the moment, and realizing that joy and peace are available only in this moment.

If we were aware of our true existence and our connection to all things, and experienced the totality of our existence in the present moment, we wouldn't seek things to help us escape "ourselves"—our imagined ideas of a separate "self." We would realize that our experience is inescapable, and that we must confront it, dive into it and live it, not seek ways to escape it.

Seeking fulfillment in pleasurable experiences will always lead to pain, since our fulfillment is coming from impermanent experiences that we wish to remain permanent.

This is the dilemma that addicts face when their addiction is taken to the extreme. They feel fulfilled when intoxicated with substances, but as soon as the experience ends, they are left again with their feelings of fear and separation, because they still experience reality through the lens of the ego.

The alcoholic loves to drink because drinking is their escape from the moment. As soon as they are no longer intoxicated they are forced to face the moment, and so they become depressed or anxious until they can escape once more with another drink. The same is true for those addicted to drugs, sex, thoughts, or any experience that separates them from the experience of now.

If you suffer from an addiction, do not continue to escape your feelings by seeking fulfillment from a substance. You need to feel within you the energy that arises when you have a tendency to repeat a habit. Look into it, see what it feels like, why it is there, what its presence is trying to teach you.

This is how we heal all emotional wounds—by feeling into them, not by trying to escape them with pleasure. If you continually avoid feeling your emotions, you will never be healed.

People who seek for fulfillment in substances fail to see that these substances do not provide lasting fulfillment. Seeking for fulfillment from pleasure always produces pain; the two are inseparable. Only when we realize our true nature, and appreciate things without clinging to them, do we become truly fulfilled. This is the experience of joy—it is what Buddhists refer to as "the middle way," what Christians have named "grace," and what Hindus call "the path of joy."

"There is the path of joy, and there is the path of pleasure. Both attract the soul.

Who follows the first comes to good; who follows pleasure reaches not the end.

Stillness

*The two paths lie in front of man. Pondering on them,
the wise man chooses the path of joy; the fool takes the
path of pleasure."*

– Upanishads

You cannot define experience, nor separate yourself from it. There is no choice but to be fully aware of it, to immerse your "self" in it. Resisting the moment creates pain, but being aware of it as it exists produces peace and genuine understanding.

We suffer because of our resistance, because of our attachments, because we wish for things to be permanent when they are constantly changing. Our failure to adapt to change, and our habit of resisting change, is only delaying the inevitable. As long as we delay acceptance of the new moment, we will suffer until we can accept that our reality has changed.

The present moment is all that ever exists, and as long as we flow with the current of this ever-changing moment, we will be at peace. But when we resist the flow and go against the current, we struggle until we are capable of surrendering to the experience of now.

The now is always present and we can experience it at any time; in fact, we have no choice but to experience it, since it is all that is ever happening.

As long as we are identified with the ego—as long as we see ourselves as an "I" existing apart from the moment—we will continue to produce suffering due to our resistance. We are not separate from our experience; we are our experience. Only when we resist seeing reality in this way, and resist being present in the moment do we suffer. But without resistance, we are free.

"Life is a series of natural and spontaneous changes. Don't resist them - that only creates sorrow. Let reality be reality. Let things flow naturally forward in whatever way they like."
– Lao Tzu

Stillness

11 STILLNESS

Stillness is our natural state of being. Stillness is being. It is the state of awareness that exists when the mind is completely still—when there are no thoughts to disturb the peaceful space that exists within us. As soon as we think about the experience of stillness, the mind is no longer still. It is a state of being that has to be felt—not thought. Only in stillness can we feel our connection to the source, and realize the truth of our existence. It is something that can only be experienced when one is wholeheartedly attentive to the reality of the present moment, when one surrenders all concepts, images, ideas, and thoughts, in order to return to the peaceful state of being that we naturally are.

To allow ourselves to experience the present moment, we must realize that it cannot be understood by logic or thought. We must be willing to leave behind the mind's need for security and understanding, and take a leap into the unknown. We can rationalize, analyze, intellectualize, and dissect the meaning of stillness for as long as we want, but until we actually take that leap, until we actually surrender our thoughts and just be in the present moment, nothing will be accomplished.

The thinking mind always resists the present moment because it cannot function in the present moment; it can only dwell on the past or anticipate the future. Living in the present moment silences the thinking mind; the two cannot coexist. So for us to be free from our thoughts and the mental prison that they so often create for us, we must be willing to leave behind the mind and experience our awareness in the present moment. If we can allow our minds to be still in the now, we will experience peace. But we can only achieve this state by abandoning our thinking mind; no matter how hard we try, our thoughts will never be able to understand the entirety of the present moment.

Many people misunderstand the concept of stillness and of silencing the mind. They hear the practice involves eliminating their thoughts and they fear that somehow that means to eliminate themselves. People who feel this way are strongly identified with their thoughts, and fail to realize that they are not their thoughts. The reason we quiet our thoughts is so that we can allow our true nature to present itself—which can only happen when the thinking mind is still.

The practice is not to eliminate thoughts permanently or to never think another thought again—if that were so you wouldn't be reading these words right now, as this book first began as a thought in my mind. The practice is to be free of thought so that your thoughts no longer control you. Then you can choose which thoughts you want to think and act on, rather than being driven by the mind and its impulses.

When we silence our mind, we reconnect with the source. The source of our being is pure consciousness. We can only be in touch with this source in a state of total stillness. All thoughts arise from this state of stillness and return to this stillness.

This stillness is our oneness with the universe; it precedes all things. It is the state we seek outwardly to find, yearning for something more, unaware that the state we seek lies within us all along. We came from this stillness, we are this stillness, and though many do not realize it, we spend our whole lives longing to return to this state of stillness and feel the sense of connection that this stillness provides us with.

Think of it like this: consciousness is an ocean; our individual experience is a drop of water. Water originates in the ocean, is evaporated by clouds, and rained onto the land, only to return back to the ocean taking its own unique path. In a perfect situation, the path would flow directly back to the ocean from which it came. Though instead, the stream is often blocked by many barriers—rocks, mud, logs, fallen branches, human intervention—all interfering with the water's return to the source. Though in the end, it always returns to the source. In fact, it never really left, since it always contained the source within it no matter where it traveled.

Similar to the water, we all came from an ocean of pure consciousness, were picked up and shaped by our peers and our environment, were thrown out into society, and forced to find our way. We too are seeking to return to the source, and because of our conditioning, we don't recognize that we are the source. And just like the water, we also have many barriers in our way. We walk around in confusion as different thoughts, people, and life situations disrupt our path. We forget our origin and our destination, so we form our own beliefs or adopt the beliefs of others who are lost, and then we fight to protect them.

How many thoughts can you claim to be your own? Everything we have learned has come from something or someone else. Not to mention that our perception is limited to our senses, and we cannot perceive that which is imperceptible by our sensory organs.

To take our accumulated knowledge as actual fact is absurd; everything we know is only a matter of perspective. History, for example, is limited to the historian's perspective. We couldn't possibly know an event exactly as it happened.

Stillness

"History is always written by the winners. When two cultures clash, the loser is obliterated, and the winner writes the history books – books which glorify their own cause and disparage the conquered foe. As Napoleon once said, 'What is history, but a fable agreed upon?'"
– Dan Brown

Much of what we know and believe to be true is based on the perspectives and opinions of other people. Rather than determining the truth for ourselves, we take the words of others, and believe their perspectives to be our own, usually with little thought or investigation on our behalf.

We are secondhand people, learning our behavior from others. The message I desperately want to convey with this book, is that this is your experience, and that you should never believe anything to be absolutely true (even what I have written), but consider it all to be a matter of perspective, and to keep an open mind at all times; more importantly, to discover things for yourself and determine the truth from your own point of view, rather than basing it on the opinions and perspectives of other people.

Most, if not all, of the poor behaviors that humans act out are not a result of our true nature, but something that we have learned or adopted from our environment.

Any negative actions stem from a negative way of thinking. Violence is a result of misunderstanding our true nature, and taking the frustration of confusion out on other people, or adopting the behaviors of others who do the same.

Anyone who acts out in violence, unless it is a desperate act of defense, is not aware of their origins, does not know about inner stillness, and is experiencing a warzone of conflicting thoughts within their mind. Their confusion inside reflects into the world outside of them, using any excuse they can to channel their anger and frustration.

What any desire essentially aims at is a state of non-desire. We seek to reach fulfillment, to no longer demand anything, to be completely satisfied and content. What we fail to understand is that contentment is a state of being, and any state of being already exists within us and does not require anything outside of ourselves to attain.

> *"When you lose touch with your inner stillness, you lose touch with yourself. When you lose touch with yourself, you lose touch with the world."*
> *– Eckhart Tolle*

What we all long for is the feeling that we experience when we are connected to the source—feelings of love, peace, joy, calmness and bliss. It is only when we drift away from our source that we begin to feel lost and discontent.

The source of our being resides within us—we just need to silence the mind and return to a state of stillness in order to feel it. When we seek outwardly for too long without returning to our inner being, we begin to suffer and experience emotions of fear, scarcity, anxiety, tension, worry, doubt and a range of other negative emotions.

> *"If the ego is in the slightest way separated from its source, it yearns to find it again. This search comes from the remembrance of unity and plentitude. As every experience emanates from the non-experience which is our real being, the me also bears the scent of its source. This remembering is awakened through those moments of desirelessness and deep sleep."*
> *– Jean Klein*

When people do not understand their true being, their minds begin to view their environment as hostile. They become victims of the world rather than peaceful inhabitants.

I'm sure you can recall a scenario in which you were the victim of unnecessary violence. Maybe someone did not physically hurt you, but they verbally abused you or called you names in an attempt to make them feel better about themselves. We shouldn't get mad at people for doing this; we should protect ourselves, but we should also understand that their violent actions have an underlying cause.

Their behavior should be seen as a cry for help, not something that deserves punishment. Being cruel to someone that is cruel to themselves is only going to feed their cruelty even more. It is similar to throwing fuel on a burning fire; you are only reassuring their false beliefs that the world is cruel and that they are the victim of cruelty rather than the victim of their own way of thinking.

"Each separate being in the universe returns to the common source. Returning to the source is serenity. If you don't realize the source, you stumble in confusion and sorrow. When you realize where you come from, you naturally become tolerant, disinterested, amused, kindhearted as a grandmother, dignified as a king. Immersed in the wonder of the Tao, you can deal with whatever life brings you, and when death comes, you are ready."
– Lao Tzu

The mind likes everything to be understood, put into boxes, categorized and labeled. It is always trying to do this, analyzing and defining everything it sees.

Though in order to experience this consciousness that is our true being, the mind must be still, fully aware in the present moment. We must be willing to give up the idea of a separate "I" or "me" and all of our self-pity and personal problems. We must return our awareness to the present moment and bring our attention out of the mental prison of our thoughts.

When you realize your true existence is this awareness, then you will be at peace with whatever happens in the world "out there," because you are not attached to it.

Jiddu Krishnamurti, a well-known philosopher and spiritual teacher, once said on the subject of being happy: "Do you want to know what my secret is? I don't mind what happens." Meaning that he does not resist what happens, and he is not attached to any outcome or expectation. He allows whatever happens to happen, without resistance. Simply because he has realized the truth that (1) he has no control over anything in the Universe except for himself and his own inner state of being. He has given up his sense of control and surrendered it to God; and (2) nothing in the world "out there" is worth stressing over or losing his inner peace over.

The only thing we can truly change in the Universe is ourselves, and by changing ourselves, we change the Universe. This is the ultimate spiritual truth: to shift your attention from being concerned with "the world without" to focusing primarily on "the world within."

"Look around you wherever you live and you will notice that the vast majority of mankind lives in the world without; the more enlightened men are intensely interested in the world within. Remember, it is the world within, namely your thoughts, feelings, and imagery that makes your world without. It is, therefore, the only creative power, and everything which you find in your world of expression has been created by you in the inner world of your mind consciously or unconsciously.
– Dr. Joseph Murphy,
The Power of Your Subconscious Mind

Turning Your Attention Inward

As one of my favorite authors, Alan Watts, once said, "Muddy water is best cleared by being left alone." So too are our problems best cleared by being left alone until we are capable of dealing with them from a strong and calm center.

Your inner peace and stillness are more important than anything you could possibly stress about. Some situations need to be dealt with (though many actually do not, yet we choose to invest our energy in them anyway), but they are best dealt with when the mind and body are fully relaxed and aware.

If you have ever been on an airplane, you may remember the announcement made before takeoff. The flight attendant mentions that in case of an emergency, the oxygen masks will fall down in front of you, and you should put on your oxygen mask before assisting the person next to you. Reacting to any situation is similar to this. It is best to make sure that you are fully at peace and at ease, before you try to help anyone else be at peace or at ease.

How can you properly address a situation if your mind is not really present, if you are only semi-aware, thinking about a multitude of different things and feeling a range of different emotions? The least we can offer to others is a moment to breathe, center ourselves in our awareness, and then help them to the best of our ability from a state of stillness and inner peace.

Our minds like to over-analyze and overthink, and unless we gain control of our attention our minds will stress us out and drive us mad. But how exactly do we gain control of our emotions? How do we cultivate inner peace and inner stillness?

12 MINDFULNESS

The key to inner peace is to first realize that you have very little control over what happens "out there" and to shift your focus onto controlling what is happening "in here" – your thoughts, perceptions, and emotions.

No circumstances can cause you to suffer unless you allow them to. It is your reaction to circumstances that produces your suffering. Once we realize this, the next step is to practice cultivating mindfulness.

Mindfulness is defined as: A mental state achieved by focusing one's awareness on the present moment, while calmly acknowledging and accepting one's feelings, thoughts, and bodily sensations, used as a therapeutic technique.

Essentially, mindfulness is the energy of being aware and awake to the present moment. It is the quality of being aware of our attention and what it is focused on – thoughts, actions, relationships, events.

Mindfulness is what enables us to be attentive to our experience, and whether our behavior is wholesome or unwholesome. It allows us to be mindful of how we interact with the world—how we treat others, how we treat our environment, and how we treat ourselves.

Buddhist monks are well known for their mindfulness practices, though you do not have to become a monk to practice mindfulness, nor do you even have to learn anything about Buddhism (though it is a fascinating philosophy, and I highly recommend that you do).

To practice mindfulness, is to practice being aware of the present moment in the present moment. This can be done many ways, but a very effective way is through meditation.

You do not have to sit in a crisscross position or go off to a temple to meditate; meditation can be done from anywhere at any time.

You can practice sitting meditations, standing meditations, walking meditations, meditations laying down, or meditations in any activity of your daily life. There are many different ways to meditate.

Many monks practice so that every moment of their life is a meditation, where even things like washing the dishes or driving a car can be a meditation. The goal of meditation is simply to quiet your mind and bring your awareness fully into the present moment.

Though meditation has gained popularity in recent years, it is still not understood by many of the people who practice it. The goal of meditation is not to suppress our thoughts or force them to stop. While our thoughts will naturally dissipate as we cultivate awareness, this has to happen naturally and cannot be forced.

Forcing our thoughts to stop or suppressing them is a form of resistance, which causes mental strain, and our attention is then wasted on straining and resisting rather than being accepting and aware.

The goal is also not to escape or transcend reality like many people attempt to do. Rather, the goal is to become more aware of reality, to be one with reality, and realize that we are reality—we are this experience happening right here and now. In meditation, we observe our thoughts, our breath, our emotions, and inner sensations, without getting attached or consumed by them. We simply witness these sensations and create a gap between our awareness and our sensations, so that we can have full control of our experience, without being driven by the mind's impulses. This enables us to remain calm and collected regardless of worldly circumstances.

Another common misconception of meditation is to visualize images in our mind while meditating. This would be a visualization practice, and while it may be useful for certain purposes, the goal of meditation is to see through the illusions of the mind, not to create them.

"It is only through silent awareness that our physical and mental nature can change. This change is completely spontaneous. If we make an effort to change we do no more than shift our attention from one level, from one thing, to another. We remain in a vicious circle. This only transfers energy from one point to another. It still leaves us oscillating between suffering and pleasure, each leading inevitably back to the other. Only living stillness, stillness without someone trying to be still, is capable of undoing the conditioning our biological, emotional and psychological nature has undergone. There is no controller, no selector, no personality making choices. In choiceless living the situation is given the freedom to unfold. You do not grasp one aspect over another for there is nobody to grasp. When you understand something and live it without being stuck to the formulation, what you have understood dissolves in your openness. In this silence change takes place of its own accord, the problem is resolved and duality ends. You are left in your glory where no one has understood and nothing has been understood."
—Jean Klein

Meditation is a practice that, if done effectively, will allow us to undo the mental conditioning that has been dealt to us throughout our lives. Meditation allows us to create a gap between ourselves and our thoughts. We will clearly be able to witness our thoughts and emotions without being controlled by them. As we lessen our attachment to our thoughts, they naturally begin to appear less frequently, allowing our true nature to be revealed.

However, if done improperly, there will be no benefit, since the mind will just be continuing its regular patterns of transferring attention from one thought to another—a "vicious circle" as Jean Klein puts it.

To get a better understanding of the importance of proper meditation practice, I would like to present you with this Zen koan:

"One day when Nangaku came to Baso's hut, Baso stood up to receive him. Nangaku asked him, "What have you been doing recently?"

Baso replied, "Recently I have been doing the practice of seated meditation exclusively."

Nangaku asked, "And what is the aim of your seated meditation?"

Baso replied, "The aim of my seated meditation is to achieve Buddhahood."

Thereupon, Nangaku took a roof tile and began rubbing it on a rock near Baso's hut.

Baso, upon seeing this, asked him, "Reverend monk, what are you doing?"

Nangaku replied, "I am polishing a roof tile."

Baso then asked, "What are you going to make by polishing a roof tile?"

Nangaku replied, "I am polishing it to make a mirror."

Baso said, "How can you possibly make a mirror by rubbing a tile?

Nangaku replied, "How can you possibly make yourself into a Buddha by doing seated meditation?"[4]

Many people meditate for the wrong reasons. They often meditate because it's something they think they should do, or they think it is necessary to obtain spiritual enlightenment (like Baso in his attempt to "become a Buddha"). The energy and intention with which we meditate makes all the difference.

In meditation, we are not trying to obtain anything, or achieve some goal. We are simply witnessing our ego, our thoughts, mental images, and conditioned ways of thinking, so that we may become aware of them, and become capable of transforming them. We are observing all of the mental patterns of the conditioned mind, so that we may realize our true being, as this primordial awareness—this universal consciousness that precedes the conditioned mind.

It is a common goal of many spiritual people to reach the state of enlightenment, a goal that is usually sparked by some form of mystical experience. Many people who have a mystical experience feel that they are to escape this reality, or that they are to somehow transcend it. Though enlightenment is not a state of trance, but rather a state of consciousness in which you can carry on your daily affairs with full attention and awareness.

---

[4] http://dogenandtheshobogenzo.blogspot.com/2011/02/zazen-polishing-tile-to-make-mirror.html

An enlightened being—a Bodhisattva, Buddha, Jesus, Mohammad, etc.—is not someone who is caught in their mind, trying to escape this reality. He or she is a person who is actively engaged in the life of the world, having gone beyond the illusion that enlightenment is to be found outside of everyday life.

Those who do not realize this are led to the path of the "spiritual seeker." They are following a spiritual path in constant search of something that will bring them peace and satisfaction, yet they are completely unaware of what it is they are searching for.

Oddly enough, the greatest realization that most have on this path comes when they stop seeking outside of themselves for peace and realize that what they were seeking was within them all along.

Nearly all spiritual teachers agree that life's greatest treasures lie within us. Though as many people speak of these treasures within, very few are able to say exactly what these treasures are. And that is because what they are speaking of is far too profound to be explained by words or confined to simple labels and definitions. Yet this is what our conditioned mind is in constant search of.

We are constantly seeking for an explanation of life, thinking that explaining life will give life meaning. Though we fail to realize that life has meaning only when we give up trying to explain it, and begin actually living it.

People have much difficulty overcoming this problem of the mind, because they insist on making life complicated. Life is simple, and becomes easily understood when we give up trying to explain it. Though people's minds are not satisfied with this answer, and they persist with trying to probe life, evaluate it and define it, failing to see that the harder they try to define life, the less definable life becomes.

Life's greatest treasure is us. All we have to do is realize this, and we are immediately overcome with joy. There is nothing more for us to obtain; nothing we need to grasp, contemplate, or explain. All we have to do is be, and realize that the very act of being is the most profound and satisfying thing there is.

We cannot know the mystery of life by trying to explain it; we know it by experiencing it. Every sight you see and every sound you hear are what the nerves inside of your head are doing. The "outer world" is just as much a part of your "inner world" as you are of it. You are a part of the whole system of the cosmos—every atom of your being is connected to the atoms of the entire universe.

The reason most are unable to see this now is because their mind is far too consumed with their conditioned way of thinking—analyzing life, judging it, comparing it, defining it, etc. People are living in their minds and not in this moment.

We can eliminate our views of separation, realize our oneness, and live as this unique expression of life right here and now, though we must reprogram our minds in order to be in touch with this reality.

We need to undo our mental conditioning so that we can experience reality from a fresh perspective. That is how we become aware of ourselves—in terms of experience. We cannot know ourselves from an objective point of view, since we always have an inside point of view—we are always having a subjective experience.

So long as we don't understand our existence as this experience in the moment, as this unique expression of consciousness happening right here and now, we will not be able to live life fully in the present moment, and we will likely suffer often as our experience will not be the experience of life as it is, but the experience of our mind, which produces an illusory filter on life, causing us to experience mental images and perceptions of life, rather than the reality of life itself.

The practice we participate in to reprogram our minds, to realize our true nature, and relieve ourselves of this illusory perception of life, is the practice of meditation. Meditation is a practice to help us understand our existence and live deeply in the present moment. It is not to go further into the mind's illusions, but to be free from these illusions so that we can live fully attentive to the reality of this moment.

There is no puzzle to be solved in life, no great philosophical question to be answered, no secret to be revealed. We are constantly in this search for an explanation of life, and it is this search for explanation that confuses us about life, and makes us think that it is some puzzle to be pieced together.

We can't explain life, we can't define ourselves, we can't translate this vast experience into limited words and numbers—we can try, but our definitions will never be accurate representations of this intimately connected event that we call life. We cannot know this experience; we can only live it, appreciate it and be it.

As soon as you give up trying to control, explain, or figure out life, it all the sudden becomes perfectly understood. Though in order to reach this understanding, we must leave behind the intellectual mind and take a mental leap into the unknown.

The goal of meditation is to free ourselves from the accumulated knowledge of the mind, so that we may experience each moment as new, rather than interpreting the new as something that is already known.

Many people have a subtle fear of meditation, or cannot get themselves to actually be still both in mind and body for more than a few seconds at a time. This anxious tendency to always focus on the future is precisely why one should practice meditation. We are constantly overthinking and anticipating the moment ahead, and consequently, we are not in touch with this moment happening right now.

The practice of meditation is simple; getting yourself to take a break from your mind in order to practice it is where most people find difficulty. We find time to be lazy, to watch TV, to read, to play on our phones and computers, but we don't take the small amount of time necessary to purify our mind, free ourselves from our habitual thoughts, and become more aware of our true nature and our experience.

With even a small amount of meditation practice, we can live deeply in the present moment and enjoy each moment as it happens, without worrying about what lies ahead or what was left behind. We then experience life without grasping, clinging or attaching to it. We are at last free to live in peace.

"The perfect man employs his mind as a mirror. It grasps nothing, it refuses nothing. It receives but does not keep."
– Chuang-Tzu

Stillness

13 MEDITATION

"Remember, you don't meditate to get anything, but to get rid of things. We do it, not with desire, but with letting go. If you want anything, you won't find it. But when your heart is ready, peace will come looking for you."
— Arjahn Chah

There are many ways one can practice meditation. In this chapter I will explain to you one powerful form of meditation that is very helpful in freeing yourself from your mental conditioning.

To practice this, find a place that is relatively peaceful and relaxing—it could be your room, your backyard, the forest, a field, or wherever you are right now (you have had enough time to read this far into the book; you should have enough time to practice a meditation technique for a few moments).

- To start, find a position that is comfortable—one where you can be completely relaxed—whether that is sitting up straight, relaxing in a chair, sitting cross-legged on the floor, standing up, or lying down. The main thing is that you are comfortable and not distracted by your body position (it may require some time and a little yoga practice to actually find a position in which your body can remain still for prolonged periods of time without causing aches or pains to distract you).

- Once you have found your position, begin by closing your eyes, and taking a deep, relaxed breath in, and out.
- Center your gaze behind the middle of your brow, keeping the eyes closed.
- Remember to practice lightly and peacefully—avoid straining or becoming tense in any way, either mentally or physically. Just be relaxed and aware.
- Do not try to control the pace of your breath, just observe your breath as it flows naturally. Let it breathe you. (Remember to breathe from the belly, not the chest.)
- Calmly continue to be aware of your breath as it flows in and out at a natural pace. Simply by observing your breath for a few moments your attention is brought back into the moment, and you are more in touch with your natural state of awareness.
- Now, as you sit there in your calm state of awareness, begin to observe the thoughts that occur in your mind.
- Simply sit and observe as any thoughts or emotions arise, keeping the energy of your awareness focused behind the brow.
- Don't try to stop or control what arises, just watch your thoughts as they come and go. Be aware of the nature of these thoughts-how easily they come, how they seem to be automatic. Observe whether they are really you thinking, or whether your thoughts are being produced as a natural reaction to the sensations occurring in this moment.

Meditation

- Do you mentally label each sensation? Do you have a tendency to name each event that happens? Do you judge one sensation from another? Do you categorize them or compare them to sensations in the past? Do you discriminate them according to your likes and dislikes?

- Observe the nature of your mind. Be the witness at the back of your mind that watches every thought, emotion, sound, and sensation.

- Do not be attached to any of them, do not judge any of them, analyze any of them, try to control any of them, or identify yourself with any of them. Just calmly sit and watch them as they rise and fall like the tide of the ocean rises and falls on the shore of a beach.

- Practice sitting in this state of silent awareness for 15 minutes a day (or longer) and observe the powerful difference this makes in your daily experience.

In meditation we allow whatever arises; we do not resist anything, we simply sit and observe. We are not discriminating this sound from that sound, this thought from that thought, or this sensation from that sensation. We are allowing all things to be, seeing everything as an integral part of this vast realm of experience.

We are simply being. We're not trying to think; we're not trying not to think. We are just sitting, and whatever arises we allow it, without being consumed or overwhelmed by it.

We allow all things to come and go while we remained centered in this awareness. The longer we stay in this state of awareness, the more we understand the nature of awareness itself, the more we understand our existence as this awareness, and the more we can focus on being aware of our surroundings and the sensations experienced by our five senses, rather than being lost in the mental imagery of our mind.

Our mind is always creating images of reality, and because of our identification with the mind, we believe these illusory images to be the truth. We create all kinds of concepts and beliefs about what reality is, what is true, and what is untrue.

In meditation, we can sit and observe these mental images and concepts, understand their illusory nature, and then transcend them. We do not have to do anything to see the truth. We have to learn how to stop doing. The ego works day and night to maintain our mental illusions, always struggling to keep the illusions alive and in order. All we have to do to see the truth is stop creating our mental illusions.

Just as a sculptor chisels away rock piece by piece in order to reveal the image hidden within it, all we have to do to realize the truth is remove our mental illusions one by one, and the truth will reveal itself.

This is done by stopping, and observing. We stop creating the mental images, and we observe the mental images that appear out of habit. A mental image of life is not life itself. People have a strong attachment to their images and concepts, and so they find difficulty in letting go of them.

Not all of our illusions bring us suffering. Some illusions can be very beautiful. Nonetheless, they are illusions, and they are not the truth. The truth that exists beyond all of the minds illusions is the consciousness that precedes the mind. Awareness itself is the truth.

The more we get in touch with our natural state of awareness, the more capable we are of seeing through the illusions of the mind, and realizing that we are not these illusions. We have only fooled ourselves into being driven by these illusions by falsely identifying with the ego.

By realizing our true nature, the attachment to the ego ceases, along with the many illusions that it has created. We see these illusions for what they are, and we are then no longer bound to them.

Sitting in a state of meditation—a state of stillness, and silent awareness—we can observe our thoughts and see their origin. We can determine which thoughts are necessary, which are the result of habitual or conditioned thinking, and which are causing us to suffer. We can then choose the thoughts we think, how frequently we think, and what we wish to give our energy to. We can also decide whether we even need to think about the situation that occurred, or whether we can let go of our thoughts and just let things be as they are (most of the time we will realize that thinking about the situation is rather unnecessary).

When we reach this state of living in the present moment, without constantly feeling the need to label or explain it, we are finally free. Free of our mind, our thoughts, and our past; free to live life in this moment; and free to enjoy our experience without the worry, guilt, fear, depression, anxiety, shame, stress, or any of the emotions that are caused by our tendency to constantly dwell in the realm of our thoughts, rather than in the present moment. We are opened up to a new realm of life in which all things are possible. Meditation allows us to realize the peace and freedom that comes from being our natural selves in each moment of our lives.

Meditation is a practice, and as with all practices, they take time. Do not be hard on yourself during the process. Just sit silently and allow all of your thoughts to arise. Don't try to stop them from arising, just witness them, whatever they may be. Observe whether they are really you consciously thinking them, or if they are conditioned thoughts that occur out of habit.

The goal is to be able to witness the nature of our thoughts, without allowing our thoughts to take us away from our state of calm breathing, and silent awareness. If you lose your focus and get distracted by a thought, that is okay, just acknowledge it, come back to the breath and return your gaze to the middle of your eyebrows.

It may help to think of it like this: your thoughts are busses, and you are sitting at the bus stop with your conscious breathing. Your goal is to sit at the bus stop as the busses come and go. Do not ride any of the busses that come, just stay at the bus stop. Sometimes a bus will come by and you will accidentally hop on. When you realize you are on the bus, simply get off at the next bus stop.

In other words, sometimes a thought will enter your mind and take your attention away from the present moment. When you realize you were distracted by a thought, simply return your awareness to the center of calm, natural breathing and stillness. You do not have to follow the thought to its destination, simply let it go and come back to your breath.

This practice seems simple enough, but try it for yourself and you will see that, unless you have experience with meditation, it will be very difficult to allow yourself to simply sit still. A few seconds will feel like hours to the overactive mind.

If you try meditation and you think it is boring or unnecessary, or if you feel you can't rest your body and mind, then you will see exactly why meditation is necessary. You are too controlled by the mind and its need for constant stimulation. Take a break, turn your attention inward, observe your behavior. This is how we become truly free.

Practicing watching your thoughts for even a few moments a day will increase your awareness of your thoughts and emotions, and will create a gap between the two. The larger this gap becomes between you and your thoughts, the less power your thoughts will have over you, and the less frequent they will be. Then you can use thought correctly, without being attached to thought or identified with it.

You are not your thoughts, and just because a negative thought may enter your mind, it does not mean that you have to accept it or agree with it. You can acknowledge it and replace it with a positive thought instead. Or even better—acknowledge it, smile to it, and replace it with no-thought; replace it with your blissful awareness.

Think of your thoughts and feelings as a river, and you are sitting beside the river on the riverbank, watching your thoughts as they flow in front of you. When you are sitting on a riverbank, you don't dive into every stream of water that passes by. You just sit there and watch it flow. Do the same with your thoughts. Allow them to come when they come, allow them to go when they go, don't dive into them and get distracted by them. Stay relaxed and aware.

When you can remain focused from this calm center of inner stillness, and watch your thoughts and emotions as they come and go, you will not be overwhelmed or consumed by them, and you will be able to appropriately address a situation without acting on impulse.

When beginning meditation practice, the mind is usually very active. Many different thoughts begin to arise: thoughts of fear, thoughts of anxiety, thoughts of sadness, regret, anger, perversion, all kinds of thoughts will begin to surface. We just allow them to come and go while we keep our attention focused behind our brow, and our breath flowing calmly.

We don't judge the thoughts. We don't attach any emotion or identification to them. We just watch them, and realize that we are not them.

Meditation is a practice to purify and cleanse the mind. Just as we shower to clean our skin and rub off the dirt that it accumulates, we meditate to clean our minds and release the thoughts that it accumulates.

In time, the thoughts will begin to subside, as we stay centered in our awareness. If you are unfamiliar with what it feels like to be aware of life without thinking about it, it may be difficult to allow the thinking mind to settle, usually resulting in a feeling of agitation or restlessness.

Perhaps the easiest way to enter a meditative state is to just listen. Close your eyes and listen to the sounds around you. Don't discriminate between good or bad sounds, just let them all come and go. Whether someone coughs, a car drives by, a phone rings, birds sing—whatever arises, allow it.

The more you listen to your surroundings without thinking about them, the more you will be able to dwell in the present moment. As you listen, you will notice that your mind still tends to create images and labels of the sound, thoughts still arise. Let the thoughts come, too; address them just as you address the noises—without judging or discriminating.

Realize that both your inner and outer worlds are parts of the same thing. They are all just one big happening. Everything is happening right now, and you are just sitting and observing this happening.

This happening, this moment, this awareness, is too vast and intricate to be labeled, named, or explained. We can only live in it and be it. It is the experience of now, something that is incapable of being defined.

When meditating, we are not meditating to attain anything, to reach some goal, or to obtain enlightenment. We are also not trying to not-attain anything. For if you try not to attain, that is also a form of seeking, of trying to attain.

We are sitting simply just to sit, just to be, to experience this moment, and to realize what an amazing thing it is to be able to sit right here and now. There is a quote by Alfred North Whitehead that points out, "It takes an extraordinary intelligence to contemplate the obvious."

We are so caught up in trying to know everything, asking the difficult questions in life, wanting everything to be defined and explained. But our knowledge of nature is not real knowledge; it is superficial knowledge. It has not come from experience, but from analysis. We have divided, conceptualized, and evaluated nature, to the point that we no longer see ourselves as a part of nature. We have taken all the mystery out of life.

We don't look at a blade of grass and see what an amazing specimen it is, we don't breathe in this air with appreciation and wonder for its ability to give us life, we no longer bask in the simple joy of existing.

We are so insistent on making life complicated, when really it is very simple. Our problem arises with trying to define life, to explain it, and therefore have some sense of control over it.

We have discussed very thoroughly that we cannot define life, and we have no control over nature, and trying to define life or control it only complicates life, and takes us away from experiencing the reality of life in this moment.

We have to learn how to be, and to allow all things to be. And to do this, we have to learn to stop identifying with our thoughts, and to stop allowing our thoughts to interfere with every single moment of our experience.

"There is an art of seeing things as they are: without naming, without being caught in a network of words, without thinking interfering perception."
– Jiddu Krishnamurti

With even a small amount of meditation practice we begin to see that there is an entire universe happening outside of our thinking mind, and that we are an essential part of the greater whole of this universe. We are opened up to a new way of living—experiencing life without thinking about it.

We are able to see how great it is not to dissect the world with our analytical mind, but just to sit and be; to look at the birds, the trees, the rivers, and the sky, without calling them birds, trees, rivers and sky, or thinking of this experience as something complex or separate.

We are able to let go of a situation as soon as it passes, rather than reflecting on it for hours, days, and weeks on end. We die to the past each moment so that we may live freely and peacefully in the present.

Allow yourself to be open to this way of living. Be free of your conditioned mind. Sit without thinking, not with an empty mind, or a mind that excludes its surroundings, but with a mind that includes all things, without being bound to them—like space. Space includes all things, yet it is not confined to what is within it. Space simply allows all things to exist, without discrimination.

Allow the mind to be like space. Stop trying to define and label every little event; give up trying to control it. But do not just sit and let it happen either, because that would suggest that you are something separate from the it that is happening. Rather, be completely involved in it, yet detached from it. Enjoy life, but don't take it seriously. Have fun with this experience.

Life is not some operation to be taken seriously. Life is a celebration, a dance; it is playful, joyous, and fun. Our conditioned way of thinking has taught us to take everything very seriously, to never be content with what we have, to always seek more—but this is an illusory way of thinking.

We can observe very easily in a child their natural desire to play and have fun, and we can feel this desire in the inner child within each of us. Yet we suppress, sacrifice, and neglect this desire for fun and enjoyment.

Reconnect with your inner child, have fun, don't worry about being judged by others who are still conditioned by society to be judgmental, hateful, or spiteful. Show them that there is another way to live, a way to be free, loving, and happy. Show them that it is possible to live peacefully, to not care what others think, and to be a free spirit in a world so desperate for power and control.

It is not often that people can step out of the limited realm of thought and into the vast realm of this moment, but when you do, you will know. Your mind will finally be free, and you will be able to see deeply that all things coexist together—all things are one.

> *"Out beyond ideas of wrongdoing and rightdoing,*
> *there is a field. I'll meet you there. When the soul lies*
> *down in that grass, the world is too full to talk about.*
> *Ideas, language, even the phrase "each other"*
> *doesn't make any sense."*
> *– Rumi*

Meditation

With practice, the majority of our time can be spent living in the present moment, and when thoughts do arise, we are not consumed or overwhelmed by them.

The practice of meditation is simply just to be oneself, existing in harmony with the way things are. It is the simple practice of looking directly at life as it exists; of being aware of one's feelings and thoughts in each moment.

The goal of meditation is to realize our true nature, and remain centered in the source of our being, and to bring this feeling into our experience out of meditation and into our daily life. It is to free the mind from the control of thoughts and release your attachment to the images in your mind, so that you can dwell peacefully in the reality of the present moment.

The goal is not to eliminate thoughts completely, or to never think a thought again; it is to not let thoughts have any control over you—to realize that you are not your thoughts, to be able to be still at times with no thought and, when thinking, to not be overwhelmed or consumed by thought.

Meditation has been practiced for centuries by cultures around the world and by people of all ages. It is not a religious practice, though it can be spiritual. It is more of a psychological and therapeutic technique for one to be able to control their mind, their life experience, and their own state of being. This can only be achieved when one is fully and totally aware of one's attention in the present moment.

Though meditation has been known for millennia, the scientifically proven benefits of meditation have come to light in more recent years. Science has now proven to us that meditation has numerous benefits.[5]

On a physical level, meditation:
• Lowers high blood pressure.

---

[5] http://www.artofliving.org/us-en/meditation/meditation-for-you/benefits-of-meditation

- Lowers the levels of blood lactate, reducing anxiety attacks.
- Decreases tension-related pain, such as tension headaches, ulcers, insomnia, muscle and joint problems.
- Increases serotonin production that improves mood and behavior.
- Improves the immune system.
- Increases the energy level, as you gain an inner source of energy.

On a mental level, meditation:
- Decreases anxiety.
- Improves emotional stability.
- Increases creativity.
- Increases happiness.
- Develops intuition.
- Allows you to gain clarity and peace of mind.
- Makes problems smaller and less important.
- Sharpens the mind by increasing focus, and expands the mind through relaxation.

A sharp mind without expansion causes tension, anger and frustration. An expanded consciousness without sharpness can lead to lack of action and lack of progress. The balance of a sharp mind and an expanded consciousness brings perfection.

To receive the benefits of meditation, frequent practice is necessary. Even as little as ten minutes a day can make a drastic improvement in your health and wellness. Meditation should be enjoyed; it should be seen as something fun and relaxing, not a discipline that is a struggle to practice.

Intellectual knowledge is great, but without an expanded awareness to match the growth of our intellectual knowledge, the mind becomes dull. So too must we not overemphasize the use of meditation or expanding our awareness. This will cause one to neglect the demands of the physical body and abandon the responsibilities of daily life.

The key lies in what Buddhists call "The Middle Way"— balance between two opposites. Practice meditation so that you may live more presently in the moment, not as a way to escape the moment. We must balance both our intellect and our level of awareness if we wish to have a healthy mind.

"I'm simply saying that there is a way to be sane.

I'm saying that you can get rid of all this insanity created by the past in you.

Just by being a simple witness of your thought processes.

It is simply sitting silently, witnessing the thoughts, passing before you.

Just witnessing, not interfering not even judging, because the moment you judge you have lost the pure witness.

The moment you say "this is good, this is bad," you have already jumped onto the thought process.

It takes a little time to create a gap between the witness and the mind.

Once the gap is there, you are in for a great surprise, that you are not the mind, that you are the witness, a watcher.

And this process of watching is the very alchemy of real religion.

Stillness

Because as you become more and more deeply rooted in witnessing, thoughts start disappearing.

You are, but the mind is utterly empty.

That's the moment of enlightenment.

That is the moment that you become for the first time an unconditioned, sane, really free human being."

– Osho

14 HEALING HABIT ENERGIES

When we first discover meditation and remember to bring our awareness back into the present moment, this practice is still something that is very new to us. Our conditioned mind still has many habitual behaviors that are unwholesome. These often unconscious habits are what Buddhists call our "habit energies"—the energies that push us to do what we do not want to do and say what we do not want to say.

Just like it is difficult to break any bad habit—such as smoking or biting your nails—it is difficult to break the habit of identifying with the ego, constantly thinking and carrying out unwholesome behaviors.

We have been identified with the ego for most of our lives, and it still controls a major part of how we think and act—that is, until we are capable of making our experience conscious, rather than acting out unconsciously.

In order to heal our habit energies—our tendency to carry out conditioned habits—we have to bring these habits into the light of our awareness.

Our habit energies and the conditioned behaviors that influence us go back much further than we would typically think. There are likely many that have been cultivated during the course of our upbringing, but there also may be some that have been transmitted to us by our mother, our father, or even our ancestors.

Cellular Memories

The cells in our bodies have their own simple form of consciousness. Plants, trees, animals, and humans all have cells that respond to vibrations and contain microscopic fragments that combine to create a form of cellular memory.

In Paul Pearsall's book, "The Heart's Code" he states that:

> *"Information is carried in the energy of the heart and circulates within the cells, and if energy cannot be destroyed, whatever memories of a life experience anyone ever had may be able to become our own individual memories. Unlike the more individual and personal information stored in your brain, cellular memories may be experienced as representations of universal, archetypal, infinitely shared memories that represent the collective unconscious."*
> *— Paul Pearsall, Ph.D.*

This information helps us understand that there may be energies stored within our cellular memories that carry with them encoded behaviors that we unconsciously act out, something Dr. Pearsall refers to as our "inner elder."

If we can bring these energies into our awareness, they will no longer be able to unconsciously govern our lives— something Pearsall is also well aware of:

> *"Our inner elder, composed of our encoded cellular memories, has anger energy as well as love energy. Most of the more angry energy is sent to our heart by a selfish brain that is motivated primarily by what I call*

the four F's: fighting, fleeing, food, and fornicating (sex). If we deny the dark side of our life energy, it will influence us without our awareness, causing us to pull away, angrily overreact, and view the world with hostility and cynicism. If there is angry energy stored within our heart left there from another heart or hearts, or by our own or other brains, it can flow within us, wreaking havoc on our heart and the hearts of those around us.

Unless we clearly read it, confess it, and understand its origins, dark-side energy can destroy our life by casting a shadow over how we work and love that others can often see and feel more easily than we do."

– Paul Pearsall, Ph.D.

Just as avoiding pain results in more pain, and trying to escape fear creates more fear, refusing to be conscious of our negative habits or "dark-side energies" will only allow them to unconsciously govern our lives and effect those around us.

In order to heal these unwholesome habit energies, we have to look into their origins, and become aware of their existence, so that we can embrace them, and then transform them.

"Until you make the unconscious conscious, it will direct your life and you will call it fate."

– C.G. Jung

Stillness

15 SHINING THE LIGHT OF AWARENESS ON OUR INNER DARKNESS

To heal the darkness that resides within us—our habit energies, our conditioned behaviors, and negative thought patterns—we have to become aware of them. This process may stir a lot of emotions within us since it will require us to face many parts of ourselves that we have been avoiding—painful memories of our past, negative experiences during our childhood, people that we resent or situations that we regret—but if we are not aware of our inner darkness, it will continue to control our lives and create suffering for ourselves and the people around us.

The darkness of our being—the fears we avoid, the negative thoughts we think, the conditioned behaviors we act out, and the parts of us that we overlook, suppress, and dread to acknowledge—cannot be healed by ignoring them or trying to escape them.

We will not heal our darkness by judging it, hating it, or being ashamed of it. We heal it by bringing it into the light—into our love, our awareness.

We heal it by looking into it, acknowledging it, feeling

it, accepting it, forgiving it, and making peace with it. Using our loving awareness, we can calmly look at our emotional wounds and begin to heal them. Until we reconcile and make peace with the things that scarred us in our past—the things that made us judgmental, bitter, anxious, shy, depressed or fearful—they will always play a role in unconsciously influencing our lives.

Make peace with your past so you can be at peace in the present. Forgive yourself for ever harming anyone, whether you did so knowingly or unknowingly. Forgive others for ever harming you, whether they did so knowingly or unknowingly. Forgive yourself for all of the ways you have treated yourself, doubted yourself, or done something you weren't proud of. Let go of the thoughts and the memories that take away your peace.

Get out of your head and bring your attention into this moment. Appreciate life, experience life, have fun with life, and be life. Don't worry about what others think of you, what might happen tomorrow, or what happened yesterday. Be at peace. You deserve it, and so do others. The darkness in our selves affects others too.

There is an effective way to bring our darkness into the light of our awareness, and I will explain it to you the best I can. This is a powerful technique that will allow you to reach new levels of satisfaction, love and liberation in every aspect of your life. Being conscious of our emotional wounds will enable us to heal the damage that they have inflicted.

When we were young, our minds were innocent, and we were free. We had no consciousness of self, we did not care what others thought of us, and we didn't feel any shame because of our actions. We were light, loving, playful, joyous, and free.

Though some point along our journey we let parts of us become bitter, spiteful, hateful, and mean. This was not necessarily our fault; we mostly adopted the behaviors of those around us, and let their darkness harden our spirit. Perhaps we even let our darkness harden the spirits of others, too.

Regardless of the transitory attitudes and misconceptions of popular culture, this childlike innocence still exists within us—our inner child is our true self, the awareness that does not judge, criticize, oppose or condemn; it just lives, and experiences, calmly and freely. We can reconnect with our inner child and live as joyously as we did as children. We just have to be willing to look into whatever is blocking our love from flowing freely.

"Your task is not to seek for love, but merely to seek and find all the barriers within yourself that you have built against it."
– Rumi

Healing Emotional Wounds

This practice, if done correctly, will heal your past traumas—whether they are physical, emotional, sexual, or result from a lack of love or understanding. By healing your past pain, you redesign your experience now. You give your wounded inner child the love, attention, respect or discipline that it didn't receive in its past.

As you go back into your past, you will be able to reconstruct situations, emotions or events that caused you previous pain—whether they happened when you were a child, in your teenage years, or some time as an adult.

Opening up the doors to your past will allow you to let go of all the pain, neglect, fears, and shame that caused you emotional trauma, so you can feel these emotions throughout every cell of your being.

In doing this, you will finally be able to let go—of every thought, regret, event, experience, or cellular memory that has been weighing you down. You will be able to consciously end the suffering and be finished with it, so that it will no longer take away your peace.

To start:

- Go to a place that is private, somewhere you can feel comfortable letting your guard down.

- Turn off any distractions-phone, television, music, etc.

- Create a space that is comforting and find a position you can fully relax in-preferably lying down.

- Begin by closing your eyes. Breathe deeply. Bring your awareness into this moment. Connect with your inner child-and feel the love in your heart.

- Look for the pain or emotional damage that has been dealt to this inner child. Try to find an actual event that took place-something in your childhood, something at school, a time when you were with friends or out in public; a time when you were embarrassed, made fun of, belittled, mistreated, or neglected. Try to find the exact experiences and events that traumatized your inner child and abused your loving heart.

- Remember it as clearly as possible-what was happening, what it looked like, and how it felt. Try to remember every detail of how it occurred, how you reacted, and how it influenced your emotional state.

- Whatever emotions arise during this self-examination let them. Do not resist them or push them away. Allow them to come, welcome them and feel free to express them freely. Cry if you have to. Let it all out completely, and then, make peace with it.

- Accept what happened, understand the circumstances, forgive the situation, forgive the others involved, forgive yourself, and release the emotional hold that the memory has over you. Let go of your resentment and emotional attachments, and smile to the loving inner child that you have reconnected with.

- Feel the weight lifted off of your shoulders, the new sensation of freedom and joy. Be happy and feel love for being alive and apart of this amazing experience.

- Acknowledge every part of your body and smile to it. Smile to your eyes, your ears, your nose, your mouth, your chest, your stomach, your arms, fingers, legs, and feet. Smile to these parts of you and appreciate them. Be grateful for your heart that is beating, your lungs that are breathing, the millions of cells vibrating on your skin. Feel deeply these portions of you and appreciate them supporting your existence. Accept your beautiful body and make peace with it. Exhale a sigh of relief, and embrace the simple joy of being alive.

- Stay in this state of contentment and emotional bliss for as long as you need to, and when you're ready, slowly start to move your hands and feet and come back into this moment.

The key to participating in this practice effectively is awareness—being completely present and accepting the emotions that arise. It may take a few attempts until you are able to stop resisting the emotions, but with time and awareness your emotional wounds will heal.

We can repeat this practice as often as we need to, and it might even help to do this at the end of a stressful day. You can look into the day while it is still fresh in your memory and reflect on what happened, why it happened, how it made you feel, and how you can forgive the circumstances and decide that you do not have to let them determine your emotional state.

Unless we free ourselves of our past conditioning and negative habit energies, it will be very difficult to live a truly peaceful life.

Once we find this place of inner peace within us—the place of stillness and equanimity in which our awareness is at ease with the present moment—our lives take on a new meaning. We are no longer bound by our past or ruled by the limits we have previously set for ourselves. We are free to live life however we want to, and free to create the reality that we desire. The practice now becomes maintaining this sense of stillness and inner peace amidst experiences of chaos and adversity.

16 INNER PEACE

*"Inner peace begins the moment you choose not to
allow another person or event to control your
emotions."*
– Pema Chodron

When our awareness is focused on the present moment,
without our thoughts interfering, and our being rooted in stillness,
within us exists an amazing space of inner peace. This space within
us is silent, comforting, accepting, blissful, and calm. The more
our attention is connected to this inner stillness, the more peaceful
we become.

As soon as we allow our thoughts to overwhelm our conscious
awareness, our inner stillness is disturbed—the same way that
moving your hand through a pond disturbs the water on its
surface. The present moment is always peaceful when our
attention is fully here and now. The only time our joy is taken
away is when our attention is taken away from the moment and
into the domain of thought.

Thoughts are so powerful that they have the ability to create
worlds, shape experiences and even destroy lives. Our entire
society is the result of a collection of thoughts – every building,
every law, every occupation, and every language or word that
exists, first existed as a thought.

If we understood the power of our thoughts, we would be much wiser with how we chose to think them. We would also be much less affected by the negative thoughts and gossip of other people.

We often allow ourselves to be affected by the harmful words of others, always worrying about their opinions and approval. Our ego's need to be validated by others is one of the major reasons that we suffer.

A thought is only as powerful as you allow it to be. The moment you allow yourself to agree with a thought, that thought becomes your reality. If you do not agree with it, it has no power over you. Someone may say, *"you're ugly," "you're fat,"* or *"you're not good enough,"* but that is only their opinion, and they are entitled to it, but you do not have to agree with it.

When someone comes to a conclusion, when they set a limit or a boundary on something—when they say something is impossible—they are setting the limits for what is possible for them, not you. The only limits in our lives are the ones we impose on ourselves.

Opinions are relative to one's experience. What is relevant to one person is not necessarily relevant to another. If someone is forcing their opinions on you or trying to bring you down through their words, the best thing to do in that situation is remain centered in the space of your inner stillness, and let them say what they want. You can calmly stand up for yourself if you want to, or you can ignore them, and internally refuse to agree with what they are saying.

The more you cultivate a state of stillness and inner peace, the less you are affected by the noise of the outside world. People's opinions, judgments, or unkind words will only cause you pain if you are dependent on their approval for your own sense of self-worth, but if you understood the way that the mind works, you would see clearly that they are still operating out of the ego—a mind identified with thought.

People who harm others are people who have been harmed themselves; they are really crying out for attention, whether they are aware of it or not, and if you refuse to give it to them it will completely disrupt their ego and will perhaps even make them think about the harm that they have done. But if you agree with them, acknowledge them, and entertain them by letting them drag you down to their level, they will have won, they will have control over the situation, and they will only further feed their ego and think that they are superior to you. It is a lose-lose situation.

The key to maintaining your inner peace in the face of adversity is to remember this very short and powerful statement: **Do not get upset with people or situations. Both are powerless without your reaction.**

You do not have to participate in every argument that you are invited to. You don't have to solve every problem. Leave things as they are, let others learn for themselves from time to time, have faith in the course that nature will take. Who knows, maybe your involvement in a situation will prevent someone from learning a lesson that they would have learned otherwise.

Allow things to happen naturally, in whatever way they like. The only thing we truly need to remain focused on is our own inner state of being.

If you want to be at peace, you have to make peace with yourself. Which means that you have to fully accept yourself as you are—flaws included. Because you are a unique expression of consciousness. The whole Universe is expressing itself in the form of you, and there is not another expression that is the same as you.

Once you accept yourself, once you make peace with yourself, and once you stop relying on other's opinions for validation, your life becomes truly one of peace, relaxation, and joy.

Think of how much suffering is caused by our dependency on others for approval. As long as we demand to be approved by others, we will forever be victims to their judgment. To be at peace, you have to truly stop caring what happens "out there" and be happy and content with what is happening "in here"— regardless of whether or not others approve.

The world outside is chaotic and unpredictable; whatever happens is beyond our control. If we stress ourselves over the things we can't control, our minds and our life experience will be chaotic and unpredictable as well. If we can bring balance to our inner being and calm our thoughts and emotions, we will bring balance to our outer environment.

The wars we experience in the outer world only exist because people are at war with their inner worlds. If we bring peace to ourselves, we bring peace to the world. There is no peace without peace within.

Focusing on our inner peace is a way for us to bring peace to our experience, and consequently the entire world will benefit from our transformation. Inner peace is necessary to create outer peace.

If we want to cultivate our inner peace, we need to practice being aware of it. We must be aware of our attention, what it is focused on, and whether what we are focused on is true or even necessary. We need to silence the noise of the outer world often—people's opinions, society's standards, and even our own thoughts—in order to listen to the stillness of our inner world.

Not only must we prevent being at war with others, we must prevent being at war with ourselves as well. This means that we must stop doing things that are contrary to what we would like to be doing, or things that are harmful to ourselves and others. We must look within and heal our negative habit energies so we can transform them into positive habit energies.

We cannot create a new reality if we are still clinging to a reality that no longer serves us. A glass that is full cannot hold more water. We have to learn to let go of our past, transcend our habitual behavior and our conditioning, and release our attachment to our ego and our ideas of ourselves. We must empty our glass so that it may be filled.

One of the things I found most fascinating about Buddhism when I began to study it was that it pointed out clearly that as long as our minds hold any negativity toward others, we will never be able to experience peace in our own lives.

Buddhism speaks of purifying the mind and our daily actions, not only because it will prevent harm to others, but because as long as we act in anger, mischief, or ill-will, we will also harm ourselves.

In other words, when we free ourselves from sin, it is not because it is what is expected of us or because it will please a deity, but because as long as we act in sin, or as long as our minds are polluted with sin, we will cause ourselves to suffer. Whatever thoughts we think become our reality.

"Resentment is like taking poison and waiting for the other person to die."
– Malachy McCourt

Negative thoughts cannot produce a positive life. Thoughts lead to actions, actions lead to habits, and habits lead to behavior. Purifying our minds and our thoughts produces a positive life.

We can continue to act in sin, harm others, steal, lie, cheat, kill, etc., as long as we want to, but in doing so we will always create a life of suffering, for ourselves and others. What harms others harms ourselves; we are not separate from the fruit of our actions.

To be at peace, we must heal all of the wounds that lie dormant in our subconscious—all of the things of our past that have caused us to act in a sinful or harmful way. We must acknowledge our negative behavior and habits, and personally reprogram our minds to think positive thoughts, produce loving actions, and create peaceful behavior.

This can be done first with the agreement to be willing to change our negative habits, forgive our past and accept the present, and second by bringing our negative habits into the light of our awareness. If we are aware of our negative thoughts and habits, we can acknowledge them when they arise, and consciously choose to replace them with thoughts and habits that are in harmony with ourselves and others.

Rather than trying to escape negative thoughts or run away from them, we can use a positive state of mind—a loving awareness—to look at the negativity and make peace with it. Acknowledge when your thoughts are judgmental, spiteful, fearful, or disharmonic in any way and smile to those thoughts. Thank them for giving you the opportunity to heal yourself. Thank them for the lesson they are teaching you at that moment. If there were no negative thoughts to begin with, we wouldn't know how to use our positive thoughts to transform the negativity.

"This being human is a guest house. Every morning a new arrival.

A joy, a depression, a meanness, some momentary awareness comes as an unexpected visitor. Welcome and entertain them all!

Even if they are a crowd of sorrows, who violently sweep your house empty of its furniture, still, treat each guest honorably.

He may be clearing you out for some new delight.

The dark thought, the shame, the malice.

Meet them at the door laughing and invite them in.

Be grateful for whatever comes, because each has been sent as a guide from beyond."
– Rumi

In order to use our awareness in such a way, we need to cultivate our awareness, and expand our awareness. This is where meditation practice shows us its rewards. It is not only while meditating that we receive benefits, but during times of hardship or chaos when we can react from a state of inner peace rather than react with automatic conditioned behaviors, or how society expects us to react.

By cultivating a state of stillness within us, we create the space that allows us to properly react to our environment without being overwhelmed by it.

It is important to remember that creating a space of stillness within yourself is something that you personally have to achieve. You have to feel this space within you, how it is easily disrupted by the energies around you, and how you can control your emotional state by staying centered in your awareness and remembering to return your attention to your breath. You can read about stillness for the rest of your life, but until you apply this information and actually practice cultivating stillness, it will provide no benefit to you.

> *"If you want to learn to swim, jump into the water. On dry land no frame of mind is ever going to help you."*
> *– Bruce Lee*

Not only is it important to practice cultivating inner stillness, but to prevent other things from disrupting your practice. The environments around us and the situations in which we put ourselves play a significant role in the way that we think, feel and act.

> *"Our six sense organs - eyes, ears, nose, tongue, body and mind - are in constant contact with sense objects, and these contacts become food for our consciousness. When we drive through the city, our eyes see so many billboards, and these images enter our consciousness. When we pick up a magazine, the articles and advertisements are food for our consciousness. Advertisements that stimulate our craving for possessions, sex, and food can be toxic. If after reading the newspaper, hearing the news, or being in a conversation, we feel anxious or worn out, we know we have been in contact with toxins. Movies are food for our eyes, ears and minds. When we watch TV, the program is our food. Children who spend five hours a day watching television are ingesting images that water the negative seeds of craving, fear, anger and violence in them. We are exposed to so many forms, colors, sounds, smells, tastes, objects of touch, and ideas that are toxic and rob our body and consciousness of their well-being. When you feel despair, fear or depression, it may be because you have*

ingested too many toxins through sense impressions.
Not only children need to be protected from violent
and unwholesome films, TV programs, books,
magazines and games. We, too, can be destroyed by
these media."
– Thich Nhat Hanh

Our mind is like soil, and our thoughts are like seeds; our conscious awareness is the gardener. Whatever seed the gardener plants is the seed that will grow. Whatever thought you give your attention to, is the thought that is going to become your reality.

If you plant seeds of fear, depression, worry, stress, guilt, shame, or regret, these are the seeds that will grow into your everyday experience. If you plant seeds of love, happiness, peace, joy, freedom, acceptance, or forgiveness, these seeds will grow into your everyday experience.

Whatever seed you plant the most is the seed that is most likely to grow. That is why it is so important to think positive thoughts, and prevent the negative thoughts from growing in the garden of our minds.

We can use our awareness to dig up the harmful seeds of our past, and to plant positive seeds for our future. Choosing to be peaceful today will ensure the likelihood of a peaceful tomorrow.

Bring your awareness back into this moment. Be the gardener of your mind. Choose to plant seeds of love, peace, and joy. Dig up the weeds that have been planted in the past. Don't let your environment influence you into planting seeds that you don't want to grow in your mind's garden.

Not only must we be aware of the thoughts and feelings that arise in our minds, but also the space from which they arise. This state is our true being, and the more we are in touch with the silence within us, the more peaceful we will become. We must not allow the world to overwhelm our state of inner peace.

If we are aware of the stillness within us, we can observe how our thoughts and emotions arise from this stillness, and return to this stillness. The purpose of cultivating stillness within us is not only to find peace from our thoughts and emotions, but to remain peaceful even when confronted with people or situations that are not peaceful. Stillness is the center from which we can remain calm and keep our composure regardless of the circumstances that life presents us.

When life seems stressful, and your environment seems chaotic, pause to take a few deep breaths, turn your attention inward, and connect to the source of stillness within your being. If you are capable of accomplishing this, you will not be overwhelmed by any circumstances, and you will be able to address any situation with calmness, strength, and ease.

> "Within yourself is a stillness, a sanctuary to which you
> can return at any time and be yourself."
> — Herman Hess

The Importance of Health

A topic I want to discuss briefly is the importance of health and diet. Most people feel that the physical, mental, and spiritual realities are separate from one another, but the truth is, they are all connected, as is everything in existence.

Our physical and mental health has a significant influence on our spiritual wellness. When we eat food, the life force of that food becomes our own. The quality of the food that we eat, and the effect that it has on our body, plays a significant role in the way that we think, feel, and act.

In many indigenous cultures throughout the world, eating food is known as a spiritual practice—as it should be, since everything you put into your body builds your cells, mends your bones, influences your mood, and literally becomes you.

The importance of food and diet is one of the most overlooked subjects in our modern culture, and the ignorance of food and health is the root cause of mostly all diseases, obesity and health issues in today's world.

In ancient cultures around the world such as India, China, Japan, Egypt, Peru and many others, eating food—particularly a vegetarian diet—was thought of as a direct link to the health of mind, body, and spirit.

In the *Essene Gospel of Peace*, Jesus says to his disciples:

> *"For of the fruits of the trees and the seeds of the
> earth alone do I partake, and these are changed by
> the Spirit into my flesh and my blood. Of these
> alone and their like shall ye eat who believe in me,
> and are my disciples, for of these, in the Spirit,
> come life and health and healing unto man... But I
> do say unto you: Kill neither men, nor beasts, nor
> yet the food which goes into your mouth. For if
> you eat living food, the same will quicken you, but
> if you kill your food, the dead food will kill you
> also. For life comes only from life, and from death
> comes always death. For everything which kills
> your foods, kills your bodies also...."*

> *— Jesus, Essene Gospel of Peace, Book 1*

It is this belief in eating living foods from nature that has sparked the current raw food movement. Many more people are becoming aware of the importance of nutrition and its effect on their well-being.

We can follow a spiritual path, meditate, do yoga, practice tai chi, and participate in all kinds of various spiritual practices, but if we are unhealthy we will always be held back from growing as our attention will constantly be distracted by our physical ailments.

When we eat a diet that is organic, plant-based, full of vegetables, fruits, soaked nuts, sprouted seeds, and herbs, as well as drink plenty of pure, chemical-free, mineral-rich water, our cells are fed, our organs functioning well, our mind is clear, and we are naturally happy and full of energy.

When we eat a diet based on processed foods, foods grown or mixed with chemicals, pesticides, insecticides, or herbicides, foods that are genetically modified, or foods that are primarily meat, dairy, and gluten-based, a huge amount of our body's energy is spent processing these foods, our cells are malnourished, our arteries clogged with plaque, our organs degenerated, our body becomes toxic, our mental state becomes foggy, and our life becomes miserable.

The food that we eat is extremely important in determining how we feel; as is the amount of exercise we perform. Yoga, for example, is an excellent exercise that strengthens the bones, tendons, muscles, and joints, as well as bringing clarity and peace to the mind.

Yogis understood that the way to the spirit was through the body. The endocrine system in our body is made of many different glands. When we feel happy and at ease, our glands are secreting chemicals such as serotonin and dopamine. When we are fearful and stressed, we produce chemicals such as adrenaline and cortisol.

The glands of the endocrine system are connected to the seven chakras that yogis believe are the energy centers of our being. The health of our glands plays a significant role in our spiritual wellness.

Another area of physical health that people neglect is their posture. Our posture can be a direct reflection of our mental health as well. When we are afraid or anxious, we curl our shoulders and chest inward as if to protect our heart. Women are especially susceptible to this in our society, as they are often objectified and taught to cover and be ashamed of their bodies.

If we continue to live in anxiety and fear, and curl ourselves inward, covering our hearts, over time this will result in serious physical ailments. This poor posture can lead to severe spinal issues and lower back pain. I myself was a victim of experiencing lower back pain due to my tendency to curl my shoulders forward and tighten my chest inward.

When we are confident and courageous, we open our chests and relax our shoulders back, as if we are ready to face the world and let our hearts guide us. It is hard to say whether our poor posture is a reflection of our mental state, or if our mental state is a reflection of our poor posture. Perhaps it is both, or maybe it is different for each individual. But regardless, this is a perfect example of the interconnection of our physical, mental, and spiritual health.

Many physical ailments are caused by psychological stress. Our bodies react to stress in a very harmful way. Our muscles tighten up, our blood flow is restricted, and cortisol is released into our bloodstream. Regardless of your circumstances, it is important not to stress, as mental stress creates physical stress.

Not only is our physical diet important, but our mental and emotional diet are important as well. The things that we allow to enter our minds—the videos we watch, the conversations we have, the people we interact with, the thoughts that we think—have a huge influence over our mental health. The way we react to our environment and the way feel about ourselves greatly affects our overall wellness.

The concept of total wellness is one that includes all aspects of life—physical, mental, emotional, spiritual. For centuries ancient cultures have understood this link between our physical, emotional, mental, and spiritual health, and modern science is now beginning to acknowledge it, too.

We cannot truly be happy or at peace if we are always focused on our ailments, diseases, and illnesses. If we want to be happy, we also need to be healthy—the two are significantly linked.

Our culture has a misconstrued concept of health. We ignore our health and even mistreat our health. We feel we don't need our health and that our minds will be fine without taking care of our bodies. This ignorance of health is a result of our ignorance of self. When we don't realize our connection to all things, we don't value our health or see it as being connected to the health of the earth.

True health is when we live and exist in harmony with our environment. To restore our health, humanity needs to return our focus to restoring our connection with nature.

"Keeping your body healthy is an expression of gratitude to the whole cosmos – the trees, the clouds, everything."
– Thich Nhat Hanh

Reconnecting with Nature

The disconnection we feel within ourselves, and the disconnection we have with nature go hand in hand. We are a part of nature, we are nature, and attempting to conquer nature has only caused us harm.

All animals live according to nature's laws. Humans are the only species that attempts to be immune to the laws of nature, and because of this, we are also the only species capable of destroying the entire biosphere of life on earth.

We can strengthen our connection with ourselves by strengthening our connection with nature. Eating foods as they exist in nature, rather than foods that have been processed by machinery, is an excellent way to restore our connection.

Spending time in nature away from civilization, also helps us realize the importance of this amazing ecosystem, and brings us the love and peace that we feel when we realize our connection with nature.

Many spiritual traditions, especially those of eastern civilizations, believe that in order to become enlightened, one must spend a significant amount of time in nature. They claim that long periods of time spent in nature, allow one to see reality clearly, providing great understanding and lasting inner peace.

Recent clinical studies have actually proven that 2 hours of nature sounds a day significantly reduces stress hormones, up to 800%, and also activates 500-600 DNA segments known to be responsible for healing and repairing the body.[6]

All living things exist in tune with nature—it seems that humans are the only species that doesn't, as well as being the only species capable of producing suffering on a mass scale. Another thing that most animals appear to have in common is their seemingly well-understood acceptance of death.

Accepting Death

One of our most common fears is the fear of death—the fear of "I" ever coming to an end. The actual moment of death happens in an instant, yet most fear the arrival of this moment their entire lives.

Our fear of death—as with any of our fears—needs to be brought into our awareness and understood more deeply. Fear is a lack of understanding, and if we learn to understand death rather than constantly try to escape it, we will no longer be anxious of its arrival. Some people are so afraid of death that they allow their fears to prevent them from fully experiencing life.

"The fear of death follows from the fear of life.
A man who lives fully is prepared to die at any time."
— Mark Twain

Death is nothing to fear, and neither is life. Yet, so many people live their lives both afraid of experience and afraid of death.

Everything in the physical universe is subject to the Law of Impermanence. Death is inevitable. It is not something our fears can escape; it is something that our hearts must embrace.

---

[6] http://greenaddition.blogspot.com/2015/03/nature-significantly-helps-overcoming-disease.html

Everything that is born, must eventually die—but they always remain a part of the totality of all that exists.

The first rule of thermodynamics is that energy cannot be created nor destroyed. Nothing ever really dies, it just changes form. Without death, there would be no birth, and the Universe would not be able to maintain such a delicate balance.

The death of a star results in a supernova, a cosmic blast of energy that is capable of giving birth to new elements. It is because of supernovae in the past that we have most of the elements that exist today.

The death of trillions of organisms, from large animals to microscopic bacteria have, over time, mixed with clay and gravel to give birth to the soil. It is because of soil that human beings exist. It grows the plants that allows us to eat and breathe, and it supports our very existence. The life of the soil is the life of us—and our existence is dependent on the birth and death of countless organisms.

Without death, birth is not possible. In fact, death and birth are just two sides of the same coin—they depend on each other to support life, as all things are interconnected.

"Life is not the opposite of death.
The opposite of death is birth. Life is eternal."
– Unknown

Things are born, and things die—but life itself always exists. Death is just another form of birth, as birth is another form of death. The death of one thing leads to the birth of another. If you were to burn this paper, it would convert into heat, smoke and ash. Its existence would have transformed. The death of the paper is the birth of the heat, smoke, and ash.

Similarly, we too, never really die. Physically, our cells and atoms will join with others to form a new existence; socially, the way we impacted others will echo throughout eternity; energetically, our energy will just be transferred—since energy is neither created, nor destroyed; and spiritually our consciousness has always and will always exist.

If we look deeply into the nature of death, really look at it, what will happen? Our individual consciousness will return to nothingness, the very same nothingness that it arose from at birth. You don't remember your existence before birth, and you won't be aware of it as this existence after death. You can't experience non-experience.

The only fear we have is of the ego, of the individual "I" coming to an end, and it is because we have identified ourselves as the ego, rather than as the one universal consciousness, which is our true self.

Our ego wants to survive, it wants impermanence to be permanent; it resists the moment and lives constantly in fear of the moment. To understand that eventually "I" will come to an end, but that our true self will live on, is to accept death and finally be able to live life freely, without our fears unconsciously ruling us.

Understanding that everything is impermanent will prevent a lot of suffering, provide a lot of understanding, and will allow us to remember the things that are really important.

The experience of this moment will come to pass, as every experience does. Life is happening so fast that our only way to live peacefully is to flow with it, dwell deeply in each moment, and appreciate it. Don't ruin your experience with fears or anticipations of tomorrow, or with regrets or clinging to memories of yesterday. Don't let negative thoughts steal your peace.

If you want to really be at peace, you have to stop worrying about what others think of you, and focus more on how you feel about yourself. Just be you! If people don't accept you, that's fine! They don't have to.

Whether someone likes you or not makes no difference, they are but a flash of time in the Universe. They will cease to exist at some point, sooner than we like to think. Understand this, and appreciate the existence of even the most intolerable of people, they as well as the moment of any interaction, will not last forever.

Inner Peace

*"Nothing is permanent in this wicked world, not even
our troubles."*
– Charlie Chaplin

The world can be a chaotic place. Death, violence,
destruction, pollution, contamination, overpopulation,
intoxication, industrialization, ignorance, oppression,
famine—all of these chaotic things occurring all at once,
one may wonder how it is possible to ever find peace.

The answer to finding peace amidst all of these atrocities
is to practice stillness. Allow the mind to be still so that it is
not overwhelmed by all of these things or attached to any
of these things, and it can then properly address them to the
best of its abilities, without being worried, fearful, or
attached to any outcome.

Do not be so focused on the outside world, do not worry
what others are doing or what others think of you. Don't
compare yourself to others. Be happy for others' success.
Appreciate your own experience and your own uniqueness.
You were born a unique expression of consciousness; don't
ruin that by trying to be like somebody else.

If you have read this far into the book and you haven't
smiled yet, or haven't been overcome with joy, then you
haven't really understood the message being conveyed. You
are alive! You exist! You have the privilege of breathing,
smiling, laughing, loving, having fun and nourishing your
body. You are one with all of existence, you are the one
universal consciousness, but you are a unique expression of
this consciousness. No one has or ever will be exactly the
same as you.

*"You find peace not by rearranging the circumstances
of your life, but by realizing who you are at the deepest
level."*
– Eckhart Tolle

Don't let the joy of living this truth be taken away by negative thoughts about yourself, comparing yourself to others, or listening to the negative opinions of other people. Don't let the little things distract you from seeing the big picture. Embrace your uniqueness, accept your body, love your body and disregard the opinions of anyone that tells you to think otherwise.

Be happy for no reason, even if people around you are unhappy. Spread your joy into the world. Happiness is contagious and if you are kind to yourself, you will be kind to others. This simple change in attitude has the most powerful effect.

Focus on yourself, your own state of being and the way you interact with your environment. Don't depend on the love received by others for your own feeling of love. Everyone is having their own experience, and no matter how open, loving or kind you attempt to be, people will only meet you from their own level of understanding. Do not get upset with others, they have no power over you unless you allow them to have power over you. When there is no enemy within, the enemies outside cannot harm you.

If we can cultivate a strong sense of stillness within us, we can remain calm in any situation. The key is to find home within the stillness of your mind and body. This is your refuge; this is where you are safe. The problems of the world cannot touch your inner state of being unless you allow them to. If we can act from this state of stillness within, there is nothing in the world that will be able to overwhelm us.

> *"An entire sea of water can't sink a ship unless it gets inside the ship. Similarly, the negativity of the world can't put you down unless you allow it to get inside you."*
> *– Goi Nasu*

The worst thing that can happen is death, and even death is nothing to fear. It is every living thing's final destination.

Everything that is born, must die—must return to nothingness, and from nothingness all things arise. When you accept death rather than trying to escape it, and realize it is not only inevitable, but a necessary requirement for birth, you will no longer be overwhelmed by even the biggest of your fears.

Our egos cause us to view ourselves as separate from reality, when not only I but hundreds, thousands, millions, perhaps even billions of human beings throughout history have understood deeply that we are not separate entities existing in a world that is against us. Rather, we are this world that we view as separate, we are an integral piece of it, everything we do, every thought we have, every action we make, affects the world just as everything in the world affects us. We are all one.

Because of the ego's inability to understand oneness, it is constantly fearing what might happen to it, it is always on the lookout for what will serve it best and what will ensure its survival, always worried about how other things will interfere with its experience.

Due to this illusory perception, the ego also causes us to have many expectations for how things should or should not work out in its favor—how others should or shouldn't act—and this attachment to expectations leads to our self-imposed disappointment.

The concept of stillness, of living in the moment, is to allow us to see reality in its suchness—to see reality as reality. Our thinking mind cannot experience reality as it exists, it can only experience its ideas and images of reality. To be in touch with things as they are, we need to silence the thinking mind and reconnect with our other five senses.

Our physical senses are always in touch with the reality of the moment, only our mind and its interpretation of these senses takes us away from reality. We begin to think of our experience, what it means, who is the experiencer, etc., all of which are produced by the ego and its illusory way of thinking. To be in touch with reality, we need to reconnect with our true selves. We need to stop allowing the mind to create our suffering, and begin to live life free from the confines of the ego.

The ego is what clings to the past and makes us suffer because of it. The ego is what anticipates the future and envisions what the future will be without the future even happening yet. Our false views of the future are the root of anxiety, fear, worry, and many unnecessary sources of suffering.

The future has not happened yet. We do not know exactly what the future holds, nor should we try to limit any future possibilities by remaining fearful of change and new experiences. Our expectations result in suffering when things do not go as expected. Letting go of our vision for how things should be and embracing how they are, will provide a lot of peace and equanimity.

How are we to know which outcome is best? Let go of your attachments to what you think the future should be and have faith that nature will take the proper course. Release the ego's need to know and control everything. Just be. Exist freely in this life and trust that nature (or "God") will take care of everything.

Nothing is permanent in the universe and no matter what happens, as long as we remain centered in the stillness within us, we will be capable of adapting to whatever situations arise.

Slowing Down the Pace of Life

Before concluding this chapter, I would like to address a topic that is in need of discussion. This topic is the pace at which we live our lives. Have you ever noticed how everyone seems to rush through life? Have you caught yourself doing this?

Our anticipation toward the future causes us to neglect the present moment, and steals the joy from our experience.

When I look objectively at the world, outside of my own narrow perspective, I can't help but notice the speed at which we operate, and I begin to wonder, what is the rush?

Everyone seems to be in such a hurry to accomplish something, so much so that the moment they do accomplish their goal they are already rushing off to the next. Our anxiety toward the future is not only apparent in our actions and behavior, but in the effect that this way of thinking has on the natural world. Landscapes that took millions of years to form are destroyed for mere convenience, just so we can continue to live in a rush even faster than before. Fossil fuels that took ages to develop are harvested and burned up within a matter of days, just to operate the outdated technology of our motor vehicles, allowing us to travel with even greater speed.

I think the whole of humanity would benefit from taking a moment to breathe, look objectively at our collective actions, and realize that life is a precious gift. The earth isn't going anywhere; everything in nature is patient and slow. Only humans move about frantically in confusion, and the separation caused by this pace of life is apparent in the destruction that it produces.

Why must we rush so fast as if to dig our own graves? Why can we not just be still, appreciate the abundance of things that surround us, and realize there is no more we really need to attain? We could all benefit from a reflection of our actions and whether or not our lifestyles are in harmony with the natural world.

I encourage you to ask yourself, "What is the rush?" Relax and enjoy each moment as it occurs. Don't race off to the moment ahead; stop to smell the roses. There is no need to live life in such a chaotic and fast pace.

"Tomorrow and plans for tomorrow can have no significance at all unless you are in full contact with the reality of the present, since it is in the present and only in the present that you live. There is no other reality than present reality, so that, even if one were to live for endless ages, to live for the future would be to miss the point everlastingly."
– Alan W. Watts

Stillness

17 COMPASSION

We are, each of us, capable of relieving the suffering of another without joining in or being overwhelmed by that suffering. It is possible to be one with the suffering of others, yet still feel light and joyful. It is possible, but not always easy.

If we do not have a strong sense of stillness within us, we will be overwhelmed by the pain and suffering of others. Not only will this cause us to suffer, but it will prevent us from truly being capable of relieving others from their suffering. How can someone who suffers be capable of freeing others from suffering? We must free ourselves first if we are to be of any use in the liberation of others.

"When I was a novice, I could not understand why, if the world is filled with suffering, the Buddha has such a beautiful smile. Why isn't he disturbed by all the suffering? Later I discovered that the Buddha has enough understanding, calm, and strength; that is why the suffering does not overwhelm him. He is able to smile to suffering because he knows how to take care of it and to help transform it. We need to be aware of the suffering, but retain our clarity, calmness, and

149

strength so we can help transform the situation. The
ocean of tears cannot drown us if karuna is there. That
is why the Buddha's smile is possible."
—Thich Nhat Hanh

The word karuna is the Sanskrit word for compassion.
Though it actually has a deeper meaning than our definition
of compassion, compassion is just the word that it translates
to best.

Compassion is defined as: sympathetic pity and concern
for the sufferings or misfortunes of others. Though true
compassion is when you are able to see another's suffering
as your own—when you are able to see yourself in the eyes
of another being. It is not sympathetic, but empathetic.

Rather than looking at someone's suffering and saying,
"not my problem," instead we look at another's suffering as
if it were us who were suffering. We put ourselves in their
position, imagine what it would feel like if that were us, and
do our best to help alleviate them from their suffering.

We do this not only because it is kind or the right thing
to do, but because we know what it is like to suffer; we see
their suffering as our own, and we know that if we are
capable of freeing another being from suffering, we have an
obligation to do so.

There is a reason the saying *"Treat others the way you would
like to be treated"* is known as "the golden rule." The
consciousness that exists in me is the same consciousness
that exists in you. Your pain is my pain. If you suffer, I
suffer. The same consciousness that exists in us, exists in all
things—every animal, plant, cell, and mineral. Right now the
world is full of suffering, a lot more than we should have
ever allowed. Though it has reached a drastic point, it is still
capable of being healed. We still have the strength and the
compassion to make a difference.

All living things need food, water, and energy to survive.
All living things avoid pain and seek love. We must learn to

evolve our compassion above the narrow perspectives of our individual experiences, and include all living things. If we are capable of preventing a living being from suffering, we should do so.

Right now there are about 70,000,000,000 (70 billion) individual farm animals worldwide that are killed each year for food. That's nearly 2 billion per day, 8 million per hour, 130,000 per minute, and 2,200 per second. This is happening right now as you read these words. Each animal is a living being just like you and me. Our minds are not even capable of conceiving such immense suffering and torture of innocent beings.[7]

To provide food for these animals, mass amounts of land are cleared, killing even more life and all of the ecosystems that depend on that life for their survival. 45% of the Earth's total land is being used for livestock.[8] These are animals we do not even need to eat, nor are our bodies physiologically designed to do so.

To make things even worse, these animals are fed with chemicals and growth hormones so they can be produced even faster. We then consume these drugs and hormones through eating these animals, transferring the harmful side effects to ourselves, affecting our own health and wellness.

We are perfectly capable of surviving without livestock, and trying to provide for the world on a meat-based diet is the largest contributor to environmental pollution. Even the United Nations has announced the environmental damage that is caused by this industry. An estimated 3 to 6 billion trees are cut down each year, most of which are for livestock purposes.[9]

Whatever happens to the environment happens to us. We are not separate from the world; we are the world. If we want to live peacefully, we have to behave peacefully.

---

[7] Lymbery, Philip. "Facts and Figures." Compassion in World Farming, 2012.

[8] Cowspiracy.com/facts

[9] http://www.ran.org/how_many_trees_are_cut_down_every_year

Most cultures that do consume meat still do not do so the way that most do in the western world. Most of the traditional cultures that consume meat do so sparingly, still consuming a majority of fruits, vegetables, grains, nuts, and seeds. They do not have thousands of established slaughterhouses; they either raise their own livestock or hunt for it.

Only in modern western civilization is it acceptable to slaughter billions of animals for the sake of appetite. The standard American diet includes meat with every meal, and as the main course to each meal. Personally, I observe countless amounts of people who consume a diet excessive in meat products. Not only is this immoral and cruel to the beings that have to endure such a corrupt system, it is harmful to our physical being and the well-being of the natural environment.

As ecosystems are destroyed, the animal's dependent on those ecosystems can no longer survive, and the animal's dependent on those animals begin to cease as well. The whole of earth is a complex ecological web, when one fraction of the web is destroyed, it affects the entire web.

"Humankind has not woven the web of life. We are but one thread within it. Whatever we do to the web, we do to ourselves. All things are bound together. All things connect."
– Chief Seattle

We, as a species, have destroyed much more than just one fraction of this ecological web. The entire planet is affected by our actions. About 150-200 species of life go extinct each day, which is more than we have ever experienced in recorded history, and it is solely driven by human activities.[10]

---

[10] http://www.huffingtonpost.com/2010/08/17/un-environment-programme-_n_684562.html

The biggest threat to the world is our own behavior. The root of humanity's problems is not environmental, but psychological. It arises from our ignorance of our true nature, and the many destructive habits that arise from a false identification with the ego and its delusion of separation.

Humans are the biggest cause of suffering worldwide. We can turn our heads away from this fact, but it is the truth. If we wish to ever experience peace on Earth, we must take responsibility for our actions and find peace within our hearts. To heal the suffering of the world, we need to heal the suffering within ourselves.

> *"For as long as man continues to be the ruthless destroyer of lower living beings, he will never know health or peace. For as long as men massacre animals, they will kill each other. Indeed, he who sows the seeds of murder and pain cannot reap joy and love."*
> *– Pythagoras (570-490 BC)*

It is more than necessary that we unlearn the negative habits that we have been taught by our culture, and learn how to properly interact with the world in ways that do not cause unnecessary harm or damage. We have the choice to either prevent planetary suffering, or contribute to it.

Each person makes a difference, including you. We cannot sit back and expect the world to change without our involvement. If we wish to properly address the problems we face as a planet we must realize our true nature, and we must bring peace to ourselves.

> *"A new consciousness is developing which sees the earth as a single organism and recognizes that an organism at war with itself is doomed. We are one planet. One of the great revelations of the age of space exploration is the image of the earth finite and lonely,*

somehow vulnerable, bearing the entire human species
through the oceans of space and time."
– Carl Sagan

The only hope we have of bringing peace to the outer world is by bringing peace to our inner worlds, and inspiring others to do so as well. We cannot have world peace unless we have inner peace—until the way we interact with ourselves and with the world is peaceful.

There is no path that will lead us to peace; peace is the path. It is not a destination, but a way of traveling. Peace can be made only by those who are peaceful. No work of peace will ever come from hatred, anger, violence, war, greed, selfishness, fear, or separation. If we want world peace, it is essential that we cultivate inner peace. The outer is a reflection of the inner.

It is truly an exciting time to be alive. Though our ignorant past has caused much suffering, it has lead us to this point in time right now, where we have to decide if we want to continue to act in fear and separation, ignore the truth of our being and cause harm to those around us, or if we want to realize our oneness, and act as one organism united in harmony, leading to a new paradigm of peace and love on Earth. We have two options, self-destruction or world unification—fear or love; we must decide—whether consciously or unconsciously.

I think the choice we need to make is clear, and the sooner we realize we are not separate from one another, the sooner we can all work together to provide a better life for Earth's inhabitants, and for the generations yet to come. Though we must do so from a place of inner peace. If we are not at peace with ourselves, we will not be at peace with the world.

The world may be chaotic, but in the chaos, there is balance. Our job is to silence the chaos of the outer world, and restore the balance within ourselves. Once we develop a state of inner stillness, we will be able to live our lives in peace.

Though the first step is creating that stillness within us. Do your part, find peace in your heart; do not let another person or situation disturb your state of inner peace. We exist in the physical world, but we are not slaves to it. Our existence is not purely material. We are the awareness within, eternally present, unbounded by the laws of the physical world. We can do what we want with this experience, and I think we all want to make it as pleasurable and meaningful as possible.

So reprogram yourself. Unlearn all of the negative and destructive habits that you have adopted from your culture. Follow the wisdom of your heart, regardless of what others may think of you. Notice when you are acting out a conditioned habit, and realize your power to change it.

Relearn the proper way to live, your own way to live, one that is in harmony with yourself and your environment. Return to the pure state of consciousness that you were before the world made you into something else. Forget about the problems "out there" and focus your attention on the problems "in here." Feel the stillness within you. It is your inner state of being that really matters. Bring peace to your inner environment, and the rest will fall into place.

We cannot be at peace if our minds are cluttered with hundreds of thoughts and emotions distracting us from living our lives right here and now, separating us from the present moment and our power to properly interact with it.

To be at peace, all we need to do is connect to the inner stillness within us, bring our awareness into this moment, and stay in this moment, without being consumed by thought.

You have the decision to use what you have learned in this book, apply it to your life, and allow it to change your experience and consequently the experiences of others; or put this book down, ignore the truth that you have discovered, and continue to live a life governed by the ego, creating suffering for yourself and those around you.

If you want peace, both for your individual experience and for the planet, you need to do your part by silencing your thoughts often and returning your awareness to the original source of your being. A source that cannot be understood by the limited knowledge of the thinking mind, but one that can only be felt by the infinite wisdom of the heart—a state of total stillness.

"To a mind that is still, the whole universe surrenders."
— *Lao Tzu*

ABOUT THE AUTHOR

Joseph P. Kauffman is the founder of Conscious Collective, LLC—a societally oriented firm that is dedicated to awakening humanity from ignorance and participating in the evolution of human consciousness. Driven by the philosophy of the Bodhisattva, he is passionate about helping others find peace and healing the suffering that exists on this planet.

conscious-collective.com

Made in the USA
Middletown, DE
31 August 2016